101
—BEST—
DIABETIC FOODS

Betsy A. Hornick, MS, RD

Publications International, Ltd.

Betsy A. Hornick, M.S., R.D., is a registered dietitian specializing in nutrition education and communications. She has written and edited numerous nutrition and health education publications for both consumers and health professionals, including materials published by the American Dietetic Association. She is co-author of The Healthy Beef Cookbook and a regular contributor to Diabetic Cooking magazine.

Recipes pictured on the front cover: Salmon Black Bean Patties *(page 19)* and Mixed Berry Tart with Ginger-Raspberry Glaze *(page 29).*

Recipe pictured on the back cover: Thyme-Scented Roasted Sweet Potatoes and Onions *(page 165).*

Photo Credits

Cover Art: Media Bakery and PIL Collection.

Interior Art: Dreamstime, Glow Images, iStock Photo, Photos to Go, PIL Collection, Shutterstock and Thinkstock.

ISBN-13: 978-1-4508-2270-1
ISBN-10: 1-4508-2270-3

Library of Congress Control Number: 2011931802

Manufactured in China.

8 7 6 5 4 3 2 1

Nutritional Analysis: Every effort has been made to check the accuracy of the nutritional information that appears with each recipe. However, because numerous variables account for a wide range of values for certain foods, nutritive analyses in this book should be considered approximate. Different results may be obtained by using different nutrient databases and different brand-name products.

Microwave Cooking: Microwave ovens vary in wattage. Use the cooking times as guidelines and check for doneness before adding more time.

Note: This book is for informational purposes and is not intended to provide medical advice. Neither Publications International, Ltd., nor the author, editors, or publisher take responsibility for any possible consequences from any treatment, procedure, exercise, dietary modification, action, or application of medication or preparation by any person reading or following the information in this book. The publication of this book does not constitute the practice of medicine, and this book does not attempt to replace your physician, pharmacist, or other health care provider. **Before undertaking any course of treatment, the author, editors, and publisher advise the reader to check with a physician or other health care provider.**

Publications International, Ltd.

Foods for People with Diabetes

Many people with diabetes assume—especially when first diagnosed—that having the disease means cutting all the tasty, satisfying foods from their diet. Nothing could be farther from the truth. Today's dietary approach to managing diabetes focuses on selecting delicious, nutritious foods that can aid blood sugar control and/or help fend off health threats associated with diabetes. Several foods fit the bill, and *101 Best Diabetic Foods* is your guide to many of the top choices.

When you have diabetes, eating right is essential to keeping blood sugar levels steady and within a safe range. It can pay huge dividends by helping prevent or delay common diabetes complications, such as sight-stealing eye diseases, limb-threatening nerve damage and skin infections as well as potentially deadly blood vessel diseases, such as hardening of the arteries, heart attack and stroke.

Watching what, when and how much you eat can also help protect you from other serious conditions that frequently accompany type 2 diabetes and further increase your risk of heart disease and stroke. They include obesity, high blood pressure, elevated triglyceride levels and low levels of "good" HDL cholesterol.

Foods that are most beneficial to people with diabetes are minimally processed, or "whole foods," because they tend to be lower in calories and unhealthy fats. Additionally, these foods are superior because they contain high amounts of a variety of naturally occurring nutrients. These can include fiber and other complex carbohydrates, protein, healthy fats, essential vitamins and minerals and phytonutrients (plant nutrients). This is important because a growing body of research indicates these nutrients can aid blood sugar control and help fight health problems associated with diabetes. Foods that make the grade include the kinds of foods profiled in this book: fruits and vegetables, whole grains, low-fat and fat-free dairy products, seafood and lean meats.

Read the food profiles to understand how each food can help people with diabetes and how to properly choose, store, prepare and serve it to maintain the greatest quality, flavor and health benefits. Take advantage of the many recipes provided to bring out the best in these foods. In addition, keep the following in mind:

1. Go for the greatest variety.

The foods in this book have some remarkable qualities and potential benefits for people with diabetes. Incorporate as many of them as possible into your diet, but don't stop there. Use what you've learned about them to uncover other wise food choices. Nutrient information per serving is provided for each food to help you make comparisons.

2. Select and store foods wisely.

To get the most benefit and enjoyment from the foods featured in this book, read the profiles to learn how to choose the freshest and healthiest examples of each. Likewise, follow the storage instructions given to help ensure the highest quality and safety of the foods on your plate.

3. Use smart preparation strategies.

To help preserve the healthful character of the foods you choose, become familiar with the preparation tips and strategies provided in the profiles.

4. Be adventurous with recipes.

The best way to experiment with unfamiliar foods— and to make foods you eat regularly seem new and exciting—is to prepare them using recipes that bring out their best qualities. Nutrients per serving are provided for each recipe to help you fit these new dishes into your overall diet.

Now turn the page and start discovering all the wonderful foods that can help you better manage your diabetes. Enjoy!

Acorn Squash

This acorn-shaped variety of winter squash is full of flavor and nutrients. It's easy to find during fall and winter months and simple to prepare. It's most commonly baked, and its slightly sweet-tasting flesh is high in fiber.

benefits

Although acorn squash is a starchy vegetable, its high fiber content helps slow the rate that carbohydrates are digested and absorbed, making it a great choice for people with diabetes. Acorn squash is rich in vitamins A (beta-carotene) and C and the mineral potassium, which is beneficial for controlling blood pressure.

selection and storage

You may find acorn squash year-round, but it's best from early fall to late winter. Look for acorn squash that is deeply colored (dark green with some golden coloring) and free of spots, bruises and mold. The hard skin serves as a barrier, allowing this squash to be stored a month or more in a cool, dark place.

preparation and serving tips

Acorn squash can be baked, steamed, sautéed or simmered. One of the easiest preparation methods is to cut it in half, scoop out and discard the seeds and bake it for about 45 minutes. You can serve the baked squash in the skin and fill the center with whatever you like; try rice or barley with pine nuts and garlic. Or you can scoop out the baked flesh and enjoy it mashed or sprinkled with a small amount of Parmesan cheese or other seasonings. Acorn squash is also a tasty addition to soups.

nutrients per serving:

Acorn Squash
½ cup cooked

Calories 57
Protein 1g
Total Fat 0g
Saturated Fat 0g
Cholesterol 0mg
Carbohydrate 15g
Dietary Fiber 4.5g
Sodium 0mg
Potassium 450mg
Calcium 45mg
Iron 0.9mg
Vitamin A 439 IU
Vitamin C 11mg
Folate 19mcg

Almonds

Although we call them nuts, almonds are actually the seeds of the fruit from an almond tree. We don't eat the outer fruit, but we get a host of nutrients, most notably vitamin E, protein and healthy monounsaturated fat, when we munch on almond seeds.

benefits

Almonds pack a powerful nutrient punch in a small package. Their combination of protein, fiber and healthy fats makes them a great food that provides lasting energy. They are an excellent source of vitamin E and magnesium and offer calcium, too. Almonds and other nuts are also known to help lower cholesterol levels. Because almonds are calorie-rich, portion control is important.

selection and storage

Almonds are available packaged or in bulk, with or without shells. Always check the freshness date on packaged almonds. Packaged almonds are available in various forms— whole, blanched (to remove the skin), sliced, slivered, raw, dry or oil roasted, smoked, flavored and salted or unsalted. Almonds in the shell can keep for a few months in a cool, dry location. Once you shell them or open a package of shelled nuts, they will need to be stored in the refrigerator or freezer.

preparation and serving tips

Using almonds as a topping or in baking allows you to benefit from their nutrients without overdoing calories. As a snack, stick with a handful (about 23 almonds or 1 ounce). Dry roasted almonds are lower in calories than oil roasted. Enjoy unsalted almonds sprinkled on salads, soups, casseroles, vegetables, stir-fries, cereals and more.

nutrients per serving:

**Almonds, dry roasted without salt
1 ounce**

Calories 169
Protein 6g
Total Fat 15g
Saturated Fat 1g
Cholesterol 0mg
Carbohydrate 6g
Dietary Fiber 3g
Sodium 0mg
Potassium 200mg
Calcium 76mg
Iron 1mg
Folate 15mcg
Vitamin E 7mg
Magnesium 80mg

Apples

With flavors ranging from sweet to tart, colors from yellow to deep red and textures from tender to crisp, chances are you've tasted only a few of the thousands of apple varieties grown today. Apples are a great low-fat, fiber-packed food that can be enjoyed in many different ways.

benefits

Whether you snack on apple slices or add them to a salad, apples' versatility and nutrient content make them an excellent food to incorporate into your diet. Their soluble fiber helps lower cholesterol and slows absorption of carbohydrates, which aids in evening out blood sugar levels. They provide vitamin C, an antioxidant that may help prevent heart disease and some cancers. Apples even contribute to a healthy smile and fresh breath.

selection and storage

A few varieties, such as Golden Delicious, Jonathan and Winesap, are all-purpose apples. But in general, you should choose apples for their intended purposes. For baking, try Empire, Rome Beauty, Cortland or Northern Spy; they deliver flavor and keep their shape when cooked. For eating raw, you can't beat Gala, Fuji, Braeburn or Honeycrisp. Apples prefer humid air, so your refrigerator's crisper drawer is the best place for storage. Some varieties will keep for several months, but most get mealy within a month.

preparation and serving tips

Always wash apples. Supermarket apples are often waxed, which can seal in pesticide residues that are on the skin. Peeling apples will remove the film but also a lot of fiber. To prevent browning once an apple is sliced, sprinkle some lemon juice on cut surfaces.

nutrients per serving:

**Apple
1 medium**

Calories 95
Protein <1g
Total Fat 0g
Saturated Fat 0g
Cholesterol 0g
Carbohydrate 25g
Dietary Fiber 4g

Sodium 0mg
Potassium 195mg
Calcium 11mg
Vitamin A 98 IU
Vitamin C 8mg
Folate 5mcg

maple glazed apples

2 tablespoons mixed chopped dried fruit
⅓ cup warm water, divided
2 medium cooking apples, halved and cored
⅓ cup sugar-free maple syrup, divided
2 tablespoons chopped walnuts
¼ cup apple juice

1. Preheat oven to 350°F. Combine dried fruit and 1 tablespoon water in small bowl. Arrange apples, cut sides up, in 8-inch square baking dish. Brush cut sides of apples with 2 tablespoons syrup.

2. Stir walnuts into dried fruit. Fill apple centers with fruit mixture. Combine remaining water and apple juice in small bowl. Pour into baking dish around apples.

3. Bake 45 to 55 minutes or until apples are tender. Spoon apples into serving dishes; drizzle with remaining syrup.

Makes 4 servings

Artichokes

Many would-be artichoke lovers shy away from this delicate, buttery-flavored vegetable because they don't know how to handle it. But in reality, artichokes require little prep work; what takes time is eating them.

benefits

Artichokes are a low-calorie vegetable that are rich in insoluble fiber, making them a nutritious choice for people with diabetes—as long as they're not dunked in traditional fat- and calorie-heavy dipping sauces, such as hollandaise or butter. Compared to the artichoke heart, the meaty leaves contain more nutrients, including potassium and folate.

selection and storage

Globe artichokes are commonly available in the produce department. Baby artichokes come from a side thistle of the plant. Artichoke hearts are the meaty base and are available canned. They can be used instead of fresh in many dishes, including pasta medleys and salads. Look for fresh artichokes with a soft green color and tightly packed, closed leaves. Store artichokes in a plastic bag in the refrigerator with a few drops of water to prevent them from drying out. Although best if used within a few days, they'll keep for a week or two if stored properly.

preparation and serving tips

Wash artichokes under running water. Pull off outer, lower leaves and trim the sharp tips. Boil in a saucepan for 20 to 40 minutes or steam for 25 to 40 minutes or until a leaf pulls out easily. Artichokes can be served hot or cold. Enjoy the rich flavor with lemon juice and a drizzle of olive oil.

nutrients per serving:

**Artichoke
1 medium cooked**

Calories 64
Protein 3g
Total Fat 0g
Saturated Fat 0g
Cholesterol 0g
Carbohydrate 14g
Dietary Fiber 10g
Sodium 70mg
Potassium 340mg
Calcium 25mg
Iron 0.7mg
Vitamin A 16 IU
Vitamin C 9mg
Folate 107mcg

beef & artichoke casserole

¾ **pound 95% lean ground beef**
½ **cup sliced mushrooms**
¼ **cup chopped onion**
1 **clove garlic, minced**
1 **can (14 ounces) artichoke hearts,
    drained and chopped**
½ **cup dry bread crumbs**
¼ **cup grated Parmesan cheese**
1 **tablespoon chopped fresh
    rosemary leaves *or*
    1 teaspoon dried rosemary**
1½ **teaspoons chopped fresh
    marjoram *or* ½ teaspoon
    dried marjoram**
   Salt and black pepper
3 **egg whites**

1. Preheat oven to 400°F. Spray 1-quart casserole with nonstick cooking spray.

2. Brown ground beef in medium skillet over medium-high heat 6 to 8 minutes, stirring to break up meat. Drain fat. Add mushrooms, onion and garlic cook and stir 5 minutes or until tender.

3. Combine ground beef mixture, artichokes, bread crumbs, Parmesan cheese, rosemary and marjoram in large bowl; mix lightly. Season with salt and pepper.

4. Beat egg whites in medium bowl with electric mixer at high speed until stiff peaks form; fold into ground beef mixture. Spoon into prepared casserole. Bake 20 minutes or until edges are lightly browned.

Makes 4 servings

nutrients per serving:

Calories 260
Calories from Fat 60%
Protein 28g
Carbohydrate 24g
Fiber 9g
Total Fat 7g
Saturated Fat 3g

Cholesterol 55mg
Sodium 330mg

Dietary Exchanges:
Starch ½
Vegetable 2½
Meat 3

Asparagus

You can't beat the nutrition and flavor you get for what asparagus costs calorie-wise. At less than 4 calories a spear, you won't go wrong unless you unwisely top it with hollandaise or another rich sauce.

benefits

With its low calorie and carbohydrate counts, asparagus deserves a spot in a diabetic diet. Two major antioxidants—beta-carotene and vitamin C—are abundant in asparagus and serve as major contenders in the fight against heart disease and cancer. Asparagus is also a good source of potassium and folate.

selection and storage

Early spring signals the start of asparagus season. Look for asparagus with a bright green color; round stalks that are smooth, firm and straight; and pointed tips that are compact, closed and purplish in color. Choose stalks of similar size so they'll cook at the same rate. Wrapped loosely in a plastic bag in the vegetable drawer, the stalks will keep for almost a week. To enjoy asparagus year-round, blanch the fresh spears, store them in freezer bags and freeze for up to eight months.

preparation and serving tips

Rinse asparagus thoroughly. Snap off the whitish stem ends and add these to soup stock instead of tossing them out. Boil, steam or microwave the spears, but avoid overcooking. Asparagus is also great grilled or roasted with a light brushing of olive oil. Cooked correctly, the spears should be crisp-tender and bright green. Overcooked spears are mushy and a drab olive green. Serve asparagus as a hot side dish or in a cold salad. Or try adding cut-up spears to your next stir-fry or pasta dish.

nutrients per serving:

Asparagus
1/2 cup cooked

Calories 20
Protein 2g
Total Fat 0g
Saturated Fat 0g
Cholesterol 0g
Carbohydrate 4g
Dietary Fiber 2g
Sodium 10mg
Potassium 200mg
Calcium 21mg
Iron 0.8mg
Vitamin A 905 IU
Vitamin C 7mg
Folate 134mcg

asparagus and cheddar stuffed chicken breasts

20 asparagus spears (about 2 bunches)
2 cups fat-free reduced-sodium
    chicken broth
1 medium red bell pepper, chopped
1 teaspoon dried parsley
½ teaspoon crushed garlic
¼ teaspoon black pepper
4 boneless skinless chicken breasts
    (about ¼ pound each)
4 tablespoons shredded reduced-fat
    Cheddar cheese

1. Snap woody stem ends off asparagus and discard. Cut off asparagus tips about 4 inches long; set aside.

2. Slice asparagus stalks; combine with broth, bell pepper, parsley, garlic and black pepper in medium saucepan. Cook over medium-high heat 20 minutes, stirring occasionally.

3. Meanwhile, place each chicken breast between plastic wrap and pound with rolling pin until about ¼ inch thick.

4. Preheat electric indoor grill with lid. Lay five asparagus tips across one end of each pounded breast. Top each with 1 tablespoon cheese and fold chicken over filling. Place stuffed breasts on grill and cook with lid closed 6 minutes.

5. Spoon vegetable mixture onto serving plates. Top with chicken.

Makes 4 servings

nutrients per serving:

Calories 180
Calories from Fat 25%
Protein 29g
Carbohydrate 5g
Fiber 2g

Total Fat 5g
Saturated Fat 2g
Cholesterol 80mg
Sodium 420mg

Dietary Exchanges:
Vegetable 1
Meat 3

Avocado

Often mistaken for a vegetable, this rich, smooth-textured fruit is most widely recognized when mashed, seasoned and served as guacamole. Its buttery flavor is a good complement in vegetable, meat, salad and pasta dishes.

nutrients per serving:

Avocado
¹/₂ medium

Calories 161
Protein 2g
Total Fat 15g
Saturated Fat 2g
Cholesterol 0g
Carbohydrate 9g
Dietary Fiber 6.5g
Sodium 5mg
Potassium 485mg
Calcium 12mg
Iron 0.5mg
Vitamin A 147 IU
Vitamin C 10mg
Folate 81mcg

benefits

Avocados are rich in monounsaturated fat, a type of fat recommended for a diabetic diet because it can lower LDL "bad" cholesterol, especially when it replaces saturated fat. But even the good kind of fat found in avocados is high in calories, so portion control is important. Avocados also contain lutein, an antioxidant that helps maintain healthy eyes and skin.

selection and storage

The two most common varieties of avocados are the pebbly-textured, dark-colored Haas and the green Fuerte, with its thin, smooth skin. Ripe avocados yield to gentle pressure and should be unblemished and heavy for their size. Make sure you choose avocados that are firm if you don't plan to use them right away. To speed up ripening, place avocados in a brown bag on the counter. Once ripened, they can be stored in the refrigerator for several days.

preparation and serving tips

Avocados should be served raw because they have a bitter taste when cooked. To use them in a hot dish, add them just before serving. Once avocado flesh is cut and exposed to air, it browns rapidly. Adding the avocado to a dish at the last moment can help minimize this, as can tossing cut avocado with a little lemon or lime juice.

fast guacamole and "chips"

2 ripe avocados
½ cup chunky salsa
¼ teaspoon hot pepper sauce (optional)
½ seedless cucumber, sliced into ⅛-inch-thick
   rounds

1. Cut avocados in half; remove and discard pits.
Scoop flesh into medium bowl; mash with fork.

2. Add salsa and hot pepper sauce, if desired;
mix well.

3. Transfer guacamole to serving bowl. Serve
with cucumber "chips."   *Makes 8 servings*

nutrients per serving:

Calories 85
Calories from Fat 72%
Protein 2g
Carbohydrate 5g
Fiber 2g
Total Fat 7g
Saturated Fat 1g
Cholesterol 0mg
Sodium 120mg

Dietary Exchanges:
Vegetable 1
Fat 1½

Barley

This flavorful Middle Eastern grain helps curb appetite due to its fiber. Fiber's bulking ability makes it a great addition to any diet because it fills you up, reducing the likelihood you'll overindulge in a meal.

benefits

Even though barley is made up of mostly carbohydrates, its soluble fiber helps slow digestion and regulate blood sugar. It's also rich in insoluble fiber, which adds bulk and speeds up the passing of intestinal contents through the body, possibly reducing colorectal cancer risk. Barley also provides iron.

selection and storage

Hulled, or whole grain, barley has had only its outer husk removed, so it's the most nutritious, with twice the fiber, vitamins and minerals of pearl (polished) barley. Scotch barley is husked and coarsely ground but less refined and more nutritious than pearl. The most common form, pearl barley, has had its bran removed, so it's lowest in fiber, vitamins and minerals but still quite nutritious. It cooks quicker than hulled or Scotch. Quick barley is pearl barley that's presteamed to cook even faster. Store barley in an airtight container in a cool, dark place.

preparation and serving tips

To cook, add 1 cup pearl barley to 2 cups boiling water or 1 cup hulled barley to 3 cups boiling water. Cover and simmer until all water is absorbed, 10 to 15 minutes for quick barley, 45 to 55 minutes for pearl or 60 to 90 minutes for hulled. You can soak hulled barley overnight to reduce cooking time. As barley cooks, it absorbs water and swells, so it's an excellent thickener for soups and stews.

nutrients per serving:

Barley, pearl
1/2 cup cooked

Calories 97
Protein 2g
Total Fat 0g
Saturated Fat 0g
Cholesterol 0g
Carbohydrate 22g
Dietary Fiber 3g
Sodium 0mg
Potassium 73mg
Calcium 9mg
Iron 1mg
Vitamin A 5 IU
Folate 13mcg

barley & vegetable risotto

4½ cups fat-free reduced-sodium vegetable or chicken broth
2 teaspoons olive oil
1 small onion, diced
8 ounces sliced mushrooms
¾ cup uncooked pearl barley
1 large red bell pepper, diced
2 cups packed baby spinach
¼ cup grated Parmesan cheese
¼ teaspoon black pepper

1. Bring broth to a boil in medium saucepan over high heat. Reduce heat to low.

2. Meanwhile, heat oil in large saucepan over medium heat. Add onion; cook and stir 4 minutes. Increase heat to medium-high. Add mushrooms; cook and stir 5 minutes or until mushrooms begin to brown and liquid evaporates.

nutrients per serving:

Calories 70
Calories from Fat 39%
Protein 3g
Carbohydrate 7g
Fiber 2g

Total Fat 3g
Saturated Fat 1g
Cholesterol 5mg
Sodium 340mg

Dietary Exchanges:
Vegetable 1
Fat ½

3. Add barley to onions and mushrooms; cook 1 minute. Add ¼ cup hot broth; cook and stir 2 minutes or until broth is almost all absorbed. Add broth, ¼ cup at a time, stirring constantly until broth is almost absorbed before adding the next. After 20 minutes of cooking, stir in bell pepper. Continue adding broth, ¼ cup at a time, until barley is tender (about 30 minutes total).

4. Stir in spinach; cook and stir 1 minute or just until spinach is wilted. Stir in cheese and black pepper.

Makes 6 servings

Note: You may use your favorite mushrooms, such as button, crimini or shiitake, or a combination of two or more.

Beans

What food is high in protein, has virtually no fat and contains more fiber than most whole grains? Beans! Dried beans are the seeds of plants called legumes, and they're a valuable, versatile addition to any diet.

nutrients per serving:

Beans, kidney
¹/₂ cup cooked

Calories 112
Protein 8g
Total Fat 0g
Saturated Fat 0g
Cholesterol 0g
Carbohydrate 20g
Dietary Fiber 6g
Sodium 0mg
Potassium 360mg
Iron 2mg
Folate 115mcg
Magnesium 37mg
Manganese 0.4mg
Copper 0.2mg

benefits

Beans are packed with filling fiber, vitamins and minerals. On average, beans contain 5 to 7 grams of fiber per ¹/₂ cup. Eating a mere 1¹/₂ cups a week can help reduce the risk of heart disease and certain cancers. The soluble fiber in beans slows digestion and blunts the rise of blood sugar after meals. Most notably, their protein content makes beans a perfect, nearly fat-free meat alternative.

selection and storage

The many varieties of dried beans are often interchangeable in recipes. Dried beans are inexpensive but require time to prepare. For convenience, many types of cooked beans are available in cans. Dried beans stored in an airtight container will last a year or more. Once cooked, they'll keep in the refrigerator for up to a week or in the freezer for up to six months.

preparation and serving tips

Beans easily take on the seasoning of any dish. Many cultures have perfected the art of combining beans with grains or seeds to provide a nutritionally complete protein. Try Mexican corn tortillas with beans or classic Spanish rice and beans. If using canned beans, be sure to drain and rinse the beans, which can reduce sodium by at least 40 percent. If you plan on using dried beans, allow time and follow package instructions for sorting, rinsing, soaking and cooking.

salmon black bean patties

1 can (7½ ounces) pink salmon, drained
½ cup no-salt-added canned black beans, rinsed and drained
¼ cup dry bread crumbs
¼ cup sliced green onions
1 egg white
1 tablespoon chopped fresh cilantro
1 tablespoon lime juice
Pinch ground red pepper or seafood seasoning mix
Black pepper
1 tablespoon canola oil

1. Place salmon in medium bowl; shred with fork.

2. Add beans, bread crumbs, green onions, egg white, cilantro, lime juice, red pepper and black pepper. Shape mixture into three patties about 1¼ inches thick. Refrigerate 30 minutes or until ready to cook.

3. Heat oil in large skillet over medium heat. Add patties and cook 2 to 3 minutes on each side or until golden brown.

Makes 3 servings

Tip: The bones and skin in canned salmon are edible and a good source of calcium and beneficial omega-3 fats. Blend with the salmon meat and other ingredients.

nutrients per serving:

Calories 205
Calories from Fat 44%
Protein 16g
Carbohydrate 13g
Fiber 3g
Total Fat 10g
Saturated Fat 2g
Cholesterol 16mg
Sodium 504mg

Dietary Exchanges:
Starch 1
Meat 2
Fat 1

Bean Sprouts

Popular in Asian cuisine, bean sprouts are the crisp, tender sprouts of a germinated mung bean. They can add a lot of volume, crunch and nutrients to salads, stir-fries and soups.

benefits

Bean sprouts offer texture and flavor for very few calories. They provide useful amounts of protein and fiber along with small amounts of a variety of vitamins and minerals, including vitamin C. As with many sprouted foods, mung bean sprouts are higher in some nutrients than are the mung beans themselves. Bean sprouts are also very low in sodium and fat free.

selection and storage

You can purchase mung bean sprouts fresh or canned, or you can sprout them from the beans. When buying fresh, look for white sprouts with a little moisture at the roots. Be aware that eating raw sprouts does put you at risk for foodborne illnesses, including *Salmonella* and *E. coli*. You can reduce that risk, however, by washing and chilling the sprouts. Never eat sprouts that are slimy, brown or musty-smelling. Sprouts should be refrigerated in a plastic bag and used within three days.

preparation and serving tips

For optimum crispness, eat bean sprouts raw. Their mild flavor and delightful crunch make them a welcome addition to salads and sandwiches; they even taste good sprinkled on soup. When adding sprouts to stir-fries or sautéed vegetables, cook them for 30 seconds or less to help retain their texture. Canned bean sprouts can be used in many dishes, but they do not have the same flavor or texture as fresh.

nutrients per serving:

Bean Sprouts, fresh
1/2 cup

Calories 16
Protein 2g
Total Fat 0g
Saturated Fat 0g
Cholesterol 0g
Carbohydrate 3g
Dietary Fiber 1g
Sodium 0mg
Potassium 80mg
Calcium 6mg
Iron 0.5mg
Vitamin A 11 IU
Vitamin C 7mg
Folate 32mcg

chicken wraps

- ½ **pound boneless skinless chicken thighs**
- ½ **teaspoon Chinese five-spice powder**
- ½ **cup bean sprouts**
- 2 **tablespoons minced green onion**
- 2 **tablespoons sliced almonds**
- 2 **tablespoons reduced-sodium soy sauce**
- 4 **teaspoons hoisin sauce**
- 1 to 2 **teaspoons chili garlic sauce***
- 4 **lettuce leaves**

Chili garlic sauce is available in the Asian foods section of most large supermarkets.

1. Preheat oven to 350°F. Spray baking sheet with nonstick cooking spray.

2. Place chicken on prepared baking sheet; sprinkle with five-spice powder. Bake 20 minutes or until cooked through. Set aside until cool enough to handle.

3. Dice chicken. Combine chicken, bean sprouts, green onion, almonds, soy sauce, hoisin sauce and chili garlic sauce in large bowl. Spoon ⅓ cup chicken mixture onto each lettuce leaf; roll up to enclose filling.

Makes 4 servings

nutrients per serving:

Calories 114
Calories from Fat 39%
Protein 13g
Carbohydrate 5g
Fiber 1g
Total Fat 5g
Saturated Fat 1g
Cholesterol 47mg
Sodium 302mg

Dietary Exchanges:
Vegetable 1
Meat 1½

Beets

Known for their vivid deep red color and sweet, earthy flavor, beets—including their greens—offer superb nutritional value.

nutrients per serving:

Beets
½ cup cooked

Calories 37
Protein 1g
Total Fat 0g
Saturated Fat 0g
Cholesterol 0g
Carbohydrate 8g
Dietary Fiber 2g
Sodium 65mg
Potassium 260mg
Calcium 14mg
Iron 0.7mg
Vitamin A 30 IU
Vitamin C 3mg
Folate 68mcg

benefits

Beets contain a wealth of fiber—half soluble and half insoluble. Their rich nutrient and fiber loads and low calorie and carbohydrate counts make them effective tools for blood sugar control. Beets are particularly rich in folate, fiber and potassium. Plus, they contain substances called phytonutrients that may help lower cholesterol. Beet greens are rich in calcium, iron, beta-carotene and vitamin C.

selection and storage

Choose smaller, firm beets of uniform size. The freshest beets are those topped with bright, crisp greens. The skins should be deep red, smooth and unblemished. Once you get beets home, remove the greens and store them separately in a plastic bag. Leave 2 inches of stems on beets so they don't bleed when cooked. Store beets in a cool place. Refrigerated, they'll keep for up to two weeks. Beets are also available canned.

preparation and serving tips

Beets are highly versatile. They can be cooked and served as a side dish or pickled for a salad or condiment. They are the main ingredient in borscht, a popular European soup. Wash beets gently and peel them only after they're cooked; broken skin will allow color and nutrients to bleed away. Microwaving retains the most nutrients. Steaming is an option but takes longer. You can also roast them in the oven until tender to develop their sweetness. Beet greens can be cooked and served like spinach or Swiss chard.

spinach salad with beets

6 cups (6 ounces) packed baby spinach
    or torn spinach leaves
1 cup canned pickled julienned beets,
    drained
¼ cup thinly sliced red onion, separated
    into rings
¼ cup fat-free croutons
⅓ cup low-fat raspberry vinaigrette
    salad dressing
¼ cup real bacon bits
    Black pepper (optional)

1. Combine spinach, beets, onion and croutons in large bowl. Add dressing; toss to coat.

2. Divide evenly among four serving plates. Sprinkle with bacon bits and pepper, if desired.　　　　*Makes 4 servings*

nutrients per serving:

Calories 80
Calories from Fat 34%
Protein 5g
Carbohydrate 9g
Fiber 2g
Total Fat 3g
Saturated Fat <1g
Cholesterol 5mg
Sodium 740mg

Dietary Exchanges:
Vegetable 2
Fat ½

Bell Peppers

Bell peppers, or sweet peppers, come in a spectrum of hues from vibrant green to deep red, depending on variety and stage of ripeness. They're perfect for adding color, flavor and crunch to a host of low-calorie dishes.

benefits

All bell peppers are rich in vitamins A and C, but red peppers contain the highest amounts. Bell peppers actually contain more vitamin C by weight than any of the citrus fruits. Vitamins A and C are antioxidants that help prevent cell damage, inflammation, cancer and diseases related to aging, as well as support immune function. Bell peppers also contain lutein, an antioxidant linked to reduced risk of macular degeneration. They also provide a decent dose of fiber.

selection and storage

Green peppers are simply red, orange or yellow peppers that have yet to ripen. As they ripen, they get sweeter and turn various shades until they reach their mature color. Once ripe, they are more perishable, so they carry a premium price. Regardless of age, bell peppers should have a glossy sheen and no shriveling, cracks or soft spots. Select those that are heavy for their size. Store peppers in a plastic bag in your refrigerator's crisper drawer. Green bell peppers stay firm for a week; other colors go soft in three or four days.

preparation and serving tips

Bell pepper slices are delicious raw—in a salad, with a low-fat dip or alone. They develop a stronger flavor when cooked; overcooked, they can be bitter. Try adding bell peppers to stir-fries and pasta dishes.

nutrients per serving:

**Bell Peppers, red
½ cup raw slices**

Calories 14
Protein 1g
Total Fat 0g
Saturated Fat 0g
Cholesterol 0g
Carbohydrate 3g
Dietary Fiber 1g
Sodium 0mg
Potassium 97mg
Calcium 3mg
Iron 0.2mg
Vitamin A 1,440 IU
Vitamin C 59mg
Folate 21mcg

middle eastern grilled vegetable wraps

1 large eggplant (about 1 pound), cut
    crosswise into ⅜-inch slices
    Nonstick cooking spray
¾ pound large mushrooms
1 medium red bell pepper, cut into
    quarters
1 medium green bell pepper, cut into
    quarters
2 green onions, sliced
¼ cup fresh lemon juice
⅛ teaspoon black pepper
4 large (10-inch) fat-free flour tortillas
½ cup hummus
⅓ cup lightly packed fresh cilantro
12 large fresh basil leaves
12 large fresh mint leaves

1. Prepare grill for direct cooking.

2. Lightly spray eggplant with cooking spray. Thread any small mushrooms onto skewers.

3. Grill bell peppers, skin side down, over high heat until skins are blackened. Place in paper bag; close bag. Let stand 5 to 10 minutes or until cool enough to handle. Peel peppers.

4. Meanwhile, grill eggplant and mushrooms, covered, over medium heat about 2 minutes on each side or until tender and lightly browned.

5. Cut eggplant and bell peppers into ½-inch strips; cut mushrooms into quarters. Combine vegetables, green onions, lemon juice and black pepper in medium bowl.

6. Grill tortillas about 1 minute or until warm, turning once. Spread tortillas with hummus. Top evenly with cilantro, basil, mint and vegetables. Roll up to enclose filling.

Makes 4 servings

nutrients per serving:

Calories 234
Calories from Fat 21%
Protein 8g
Carbohydrate 41g
Fiber 14g
Total Fat 6g

Saturated Fat 1g
Cholesterol 0mg
Sodium 340mg

Dietary Exchanges:
Vegetable 2
Starch 2
Fat 1

Black-Eyed Peas

Tradition suggests eating black-eyed peas on New Year's Day will bring good fortune in the coming year. This legendary luck-bearing legume is easy to spot, with the characteristic "black eye" in its bean-shaped inner curve.

benefits

Black-eyed peas, also called cowpeas, bring a winning combination of fiber and protein to a diabetic diet, helping to fill you up and keep your hunger in check between meals. The fiber is mostly soluble, so it helps lower cholesterol and regulate blood sugar. Not only are black-eyed peas very low in fat, they have fewer calories and carbohydrates than other legumes. They provide respectable amounts of calcium, iron, potassium and folate, too.

selection and storage

In some areas, you may find fresh black-eyed peas in season. Store them in a plastic bag in your refrigerator's vegetable drawer and use them within a week. If fresh aren't available, dried, canned and frozen are nutritious alternatives. If you opt for dried black-eyed peas, look for ones that have some shine. If using canned, choose a variety with no salt added or drain and rinse the beans under cool water.

preparation and serving tips

Black-eyed peas can be used in soups or casseroles or served as a side dish. They are the primary ingredient in the traditional New Year's Hoppin' John, which includes bacon or other high-fat ingredients, so try and use lower-fat alternatives when serving up this savory dish. Dried black-eyed peas should be soaked overnight before cooking. Canned varieties may be too soft for some recipes.

nutrients per serving:

**Black-Eyed Peas
½ cup cooked**

Calories 80
Protein 3g
Total Fat 0g
Saturated Fat 0g
Cholesterol 0g
Carbohydrate 17g
Dietary Fiber 4g
Sodium 0mg
Potassium 345mg
Calcium 106mg
Iron 0.9mg
Vitamin A 653 IU
Vitamin C 2mg
Folate 105mcg

black-eyed pea and chicken salad

2½ cups chopped cooked chicken
1 can (about 15 ounces) black-eyed peas,
    rinsed and drained, *or* 1½ cups fresh
    or frozen black-eyed peas, cooked
    and drained
1 cup chopped celery
1 cup chopped green and yellow bell
    peppers
½ cup chopped red onion
¼ cup low-fat mayonnaise
¼ cup plain nonfat yogurt
1 pickled jalapeño pepper,* drained,
    seeded and minced
1 teaspoon pickled jalapeño juice
¼ teaspoon salt
    Red bell peppers, halved and seeded
    (optional)
    Chopped fresh parsley (optional)

*Jalapeño peppers can sting and irritate the skin,
so wear rubber gloves when handling peppers and
do not touch your eyes.*

nutrients per serving:

Calories 259
Calories from Fat 24%
Protein 27g
Carbohydrate 20g
Fiber 4g

Total Fat 7g
Saturated Fat 2g
Cholesterol 73mg
Sodium 459mg

Dietary Exchanges:
Vegetable 1
Starch 1
Meat 3

1. Combine chicken, black-eyed peas, celery, chopped bell peppers and onion in large bowl; mix gently.

2. Combine mayonnaise, yogurt, jalapeño pepper, jalapeño juice and salt in small bowl; mix well. Spoon over chicken mixture; toss to coat.

3. Spoon salad into red bell peppers and top with parsley, if desired. *Makes 4 servings*

Blackberries

Blackberries are a wonder food. When fully ripe, they are sweet and juicy, yet they are low in calories and high in fiber. They are great for baking or just eating out of hand.

benefits

A handful of blackberries has more fiber than a serving of some whole grain cereals. They are packed with soluble fiber, which slows absorption of sugar and helps steady blood sugar levels. Their nearly black appearance comes from high levels of anthocyanins and ellagic acid, two phytonutrients with numerous health benefits, such as helping to prevent heart disease and cancer and combating aging. Fresh blackberries are also an excellent source of vitamin C.

selection and storage

Look for berries that are glossy, deep-colored, plump, well-rounded and firm. The darker the berries, the riper and sweeter they are. Refrigerate blackberries, but don't wash them until you're ready to eat them, or they can get moldy. They are best if used within two days. To enjoy fresh blackberries year-round, place washed and dried berries in a single layer on a cookie sheet in the freezer; once frozen, place them in an airtight container and thaw as needed.

preparation and serving tips

Wash blackberries gently under cool running water, drain well and pick through to remove stems and berries that are too soft. Do not overhandle them, or their cells will break open and they will lose juice and nutrients. Enjoy fresh blackberries alone, over cereal or yogurt or with a refreshing scoop of sorbet.

nutrients per serving:

Blackberries
½ cup

Calories 31
Protein 1g
Total Fat 0g
Saturated Fat 0g

Cholesterol 0g
Carbohydrate 7g
Dietary Fiber 4g
Sodium 0mg
Potassium 120mg
Calcium 21mg

Iron 0.5mg
Vitamin A 154 IU
Vitamin C 15mg
Folate 18mcg

mixed berry tart with ginger-raspberry glaze

1 refrigerated pie crust, at room
  temperature
¾ cup no-sugar-added seedless raspberry
  fruit spread
½ teaspoon grated fresh ginger *or*
  ¼ teaspoon ground ginger
2 cups fresh or thawed frozen blueberries
2 cups fresh or thawed frozen blackberries
1 medium peach, peeled and thinly sliced

1. Preheat oven to 450°F. Coat 9-inch pie pan
or tart pan with nonstick cooking spray.

2. Carefully place pie crust on bottom of pan.
Turn edge of pie crust inward to form
½-inch-thick edge. Press edge firmly against
side of pan. Pierce dough on bottom of pan
all over with fork. Bake 12 minutes or until
golden brown. Cool completely on wire rack.

3. Meanwhile, heat fruit spread in small
saucepan over high heat; stir until completely
melted. Immediately remove from heat; stir
in ginger. Cool slightly. Place 2 tablespoons
glaze in small bowl.

4. Combine blueberries, blackberries and
remaining glaze in large bowl.

5. Brush reserved 2 tablespoons glaze evenly
over bottom of cooled crust. Arrange peach
slices on top of crust; mound mixed berries
on top of peach slices. Refrigerate at least
2 hours before serving.   *Makes 8 servings*

nutrients per serving:

Calories 191
Calories from Fat 33%
Protein 1g
Carbohydrate 32g
Fiber 3g
Total Fat 7g
Saturated Fat 3g
Cholesterol 5mg
Sodium 172mg

Dietary Exchanges:
Fruit 1
Starch 1
Fat 1½

Blueberries

Blueberries are antioxidant superstars, ranking second among top antioxidant-rich foods. Great for your eyes, memory and heart, these flavorful berries are a true health bargain.

benefits

Antioxidants in blueberries may protect your eyes and brain cells and help reverse age-related memory loss. Besides being packed with antioxidants, blueberries are a good source of fiber and provide vitamin C and iron. Recent research suggests that eating blueberries as part of a healthy diet may help reduce several key risk factors for cardiovascular disease and diabetes, such as accumulation of belly fat, high blood cholesterol and high blood sugar.

selection and storage

Blueberries are at their best when they are in season—from May through October. Choose blueberries that are firm, uniform in size and indigo blue with a silvery frost. Sort and discard shriveled or moldy berries, but do not wash blueberries until you're ready to use them. Store them in a moisture-proof container in the refrigerator for up to five days. Freeze washed and dried blueberries in a single layer on a cookie sheet, and place in a sealed bag or container once frozen.

preparation and serving tips

Enjoy blueberries on cereal or yogurt, in salads, with a splash of cream or simply out of hand. Use blueberries to make jam for a nutritious low-fat spread for toast or crackers. Frozen blueberries make a refreshing snack on a hot day and are a great addition to smoothies. Frozen blueberries are best used in baking, but keep in mind they become mushy once thawed. Blueberries are easy to bake into muffins, pancakes, quick breads, pies, cobblers and fruit crisps.

nutrients per serving:

Blueberries
½ cup

Calories 42
Protein 1g
Total Fat 0g
Saturated Fat 0g
Cholesterol 0g
Carbohydrate 11g
Dietary Fiber 2g

Sodium 0mg
Potassium 60mg
Calcium 4mg
Iron 0.2mg
Vitamin A 40 IU
Vitamin C 7mg
Folate 4mcg

snacking surprise muffins

- 1½ cups all-purpose flour
- 1 cup fresh or frozen blueberries
- ½ cup sugar
- 2½ teaspoons baking powder
- 1 teaspoon ground cinnamon
- ¼ teaspoon salt
- ⅔ cup buttermilk
- ¼ cup (½ stick) butter, melted
- 1 egg, beaten
- 3 tablespoons peach preserves

Topping

- 1 tablespoon sugar
- ¼ teaspoon ground cinnamon

1. Preheat oven to 400°F. Line 12 standard (2½-inch) muffin cups with paper baking cups.

2. Combine flour, blueberries, ½ cup sugar, baking powder, 1 teaspoon cinnamon and salt in medium bowl. Combine buttermilk, butter and egg in small bowl. Add to flour mixture; mix just until moistened.

3. Spoon about 1 tablespoon batter into each muffin cup. Drop scant teaspoonful preserves into center of batter in each cup; evenly top with remaining batter.

4. Combine 1 tablespoon sugar and ¼ teaspoon cinnamon in small bowl; sprinkle evenly over batter.

5. Bake 18 to 20 minutes or until lightly browned. Remove to wire rack to cool completely.

Makes 12 servings

nutrients per serving:

Calories 156
Calories from Fat 26%
Protein 3g
Carbohydrate 27g
Fiber 1g
Total Fat 5g
Saturated Fat 1g
Cholesterol 18mg
Sodium 215mg

Dietary Exchanges:
Starch 1½
Fat 1

Broccoli

Whether eaten raw or cooked, you are truly getting a powerhouse of nutrients when you incorporate this cruciferous vegetable into your diet.

nutrients per serving:

Broccoli
½ cup cooked

Calories 27
Protein 2g
Total Fat 0g
Saturated Fat 0g
Cholesterol 0g
Carbohydrate 6g
Dietary Fiber 3g
Sodium 32mg
Potassium 229mg
Calcium 31mg
Iron 0.5mg
Vitamin A 1,207 IU
Vitamin C 51mg
Folate 84mcg

benefits

In addition to being low in fat and calories, broccoli is one of the vegetables lowest in sugars and carbohydrates. Broccoli's noteworthy nutrients include vitamin C, vitamin A (mostly as beta-carotene), folate, calcium and fiber. And it is rich in an array of phytonutrients that serve as powerful cancer fighters, helping to inhibit tumor growth and boost the action of protective enzymes.

selection and storage

Look for broccoli that's dark green or even purplish green but not yellow. Florets should be compact and of even color. Leaves should not be wilted and stalks should not be fat and woody. The greener it is, the more beta-carotene it has. Store broccoli unwashed in a plastic bag in the crisper drawer in the refrigerator and use within a few days.

preparation and serving tips

Wash broccoli just before using. Steaming is the best way to retain broccoli's nutrients. Steam only until crisp-tender, about 5 minutes. Overcooking broccoli will produce an unpleasant odor. Broccoli florets can boost the texture, flavor and color of any stir-fry dish. Raw broccoli tossed into salads boosts the nutrition of a midday meal. And it makes great finger food to use as a snack with a low-fat dip. As a side dish, skip the cheese sauce; instead, add lemon juice, cracked pepper and a drizzle of olive oil.

Broccoli Rabe

The Italians have been eating broccoli rabe for years, but it has only recently become mainstream due to its nutritional benefits and savory qualities. This vegetable, closely related to turnips and cabbage (not broccoli), is also known as broccoli raab or rapini.

benefits

Like its cruciferous-vegetable relatives, broccoli rabe supplies a hefty dose of health-promoting nutrients. It is great for people with diabetes as it is low in calories and carbohydrates. Just 1/2 cup provides more than 10 percent of the recommended daily amounts of fiber, potassium, folate and calcium and more than 50 percent of daily needs for vitamins A and C. Plus, it's packed with powerful cancer-fighting phytonutrients.

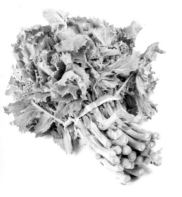

selection and storage

Broccoli rabe can be found from fall to spring in markets with specialty produce sections. Look for broccoli rabe that is bright green with firm, crisp leaves, broccoli-like buds and thin stalks, free of yellowing and spotting. Wrap loosely in a plastic bag and refrigerate for up to five days. After cooking, refrigerate leftovers in a sealed container for no more than two days.

preparation and serving tips

This bitter green may be an acquired taste. If you find the flavor too strong, blanch it in boiling water for 30 to 60 seconds before cooking. Because it's tough, broccoli rabe is usually steamed or sautéed. Remove an inch from each stem and peel the lower half of thick stems to reduce toughness.

Broccoli rabe can easily complement heavy, spiced entrées. Or sauté it in olive oil with red pepper flakes and minced garlic and serve alone.

nutrients per serving:

Broccoli Rabe
1/2 cup cooked

Calories 38
Protein 4g
Total Fat 0.5g
Saturated Fat 0g
Cholesterol 0g
Carbohydrate 4g
Dietary Fiber 3g
Sodium 64mg
Potassium 390mg
Calcium 136mg
Iron 1.5mg
Vitamin A 5,213 IU
Vitamin C 43mg
Folate 82mcg

Brown Rice

Brown rice is a pantry staple for those with diabetes. Not only it is nutritionally superior to white rice, it has a nuttier flavor and chewier texture from its natural bran coating.

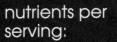

nutrients per serving:

Brown Rice, long grain
½ cup cooked

Calories 108
Protein 3g
Total Fat 1g
Saturated Fat 0g
Cholesterol 0g
Carbohydrate 22g
Dietary Fiber 2g
Sodium 5mg
Potassium 40mg
Iron 0.4mg
Magnesium 42mg
Phosphorus 81mg
Manganese 0.9mg
Selenium 9.6mcg

benefits

Brown rice is considered a whole grain, so it's an excellent source of complex carbohydrates, especially fiber. In fact, it has three times the fiber of the ever-so-popular white rice. And while some white rice is enriched to add back nutrients that are lost when the bran is removed during the refining process, brown rice still naturally contains more magnesium, phosphorus, manganese and selenium. Research has shown that brown rice helps regulate glucose metabolism in people with diabetes, likely due to its high fiber and mineral contents.

selection and storage

Brown rice is more perishable than white rice and keeps about six months if refrigerated. It is available in several forms: regular brown rice in long and short grain; quick brown rice, which has been partially cooked and dehydrated; and instant brown rice, which has been fully cooked and dehydrated. The main difference among the varieties is cooking time.

preparation and serving tips

Long grain brown rice takes about 30 minutes to cook; short grain brown rice takes about 40 minutes. Instant and quick-cooking varieties cook in 10 to 15 minutes. For tasty, satisfying and nutrient-rich meals, serve brown rice with stir-fries and other mixed dishes that include plenty of vegetables and lean meat or tofu. Or try a cool rice salad with peas, red bell peppers and a warm low-fat vinaigrette dressing.

stuffed bell peppers

1 cup chopped fresh tomatoes
1 jalapeño pepper,* seeded and chopped
   (optional)
1 teaspoon chopped fresh cilantro
½ clove garlic, finely minced
½ teaspoon dried oregano
¼ teaspoon ground cumin
6 ounces 95% lean ground beef
½ cup cooked brown rice
¼ cup cholesterol-free egg substitute
   or 2 egg whites
2 tablespoons finely chopped onion
¼ teaspoon salt
⅛ teaspoon black pepper
2 large bell peppers, any color, cut in
   half lengthwise and seeded

*Jalapeño peppers can sting and irritate the skin, so wear rubber gloves when handling peppers and do not touch your eyes.

1. Preheat oven to 400°F. Spray four 12×12-inch sheets heavy-duty foil with nonstick cooking spray.

2. Combine tomatoes, jalapeño pepper, if desired, cilantro, garlic, oregano and cumin in small bowl.

3. Combine beef, rice, egg substitute, onion, salt and black pepper in large bowl; mix well. Stir in ⅔ cup tomato mixture. Spoon filling evenly into bell pepper halves.

4. Place each pepper half on prepared foil sheet. Double fold sides and ends of foil to seal packets. Place packets on baking sheet.

5. Bake 45 minutes or until meat is browned and vegetables are tender. Carefully open one end of each packet to allow steam to escape. Open packets and transfer pepper halves to serving plates. Serve with remaining tomato mixture.
Makes 4 servings

nutrients per serving:

Calories 158
Calories from Fat 40%
Protein 11g
Carbohydrate 13g
Fiber 2g
Total Fat 7g
Saturated Fat 3g

Cholesterol 29mg
Sodium 205mg

Dietary Exchanges:
Vegetable 2½
Meat 1½

Brussels Sprouts

Possibly one of the least preferred of the vegetables, these little cabbage look-alikes belong to the cabbage family—and they share many of the same health benefits.

nutrients per serving:

Brussels Sprouts
½ cup cooked

Calories 28
Protein 2g
Total Fat 0g
Saturated Fat 0g
Cholesterol 0g
Carbohydrate 6g
Dietary Fiber 2g
Sodium 15mg
Potassium 245mg
Calcium 28mg
Iron 0.9mg
Vitamin A 604 IU
Vitamin C 48mg
Folate 47mcg

benefits

Brussels sprouts are a good choice for a diabetic diet, with fiber to help regulate blood sugar but low levels of carbohydrates that are known to boost blood sugar. They're naturally low in fat but, unlike many vegetables, rather high in protein. You can make the protein the main component of a meal by serving brussels sprouts with whole grains, such as barley or brown rice, and skipping higher-fat protein sources like meat.

selection and storage

Fall and winter are brussels sprouts seasons. Look for a pronounced green color and tight, compact, firm heads. The fewer yellowed, wilted or loose leaves the better. Opt for smaller heads, which are more tender and flavorful. Choose those of similar size so they cook at the same rate. Brussels sprouts will last a week or two stored in a loosely closed plastic bag in the refrigerator.

preparation and serving tips

Rinse brussels sprouts under running water, pull off loose or wilted leaves and trim the stem ends. Cut an "X" in the bottom of the stems to help the sprouts cook more evenly. To preserve nutrients and minimize odor, steam rather than boil your brussels sprouts and cook just until tender. They can be roasted, too: Cut in half lengthwise, toss with olive oil, salt and pepper and roast in a 400°F oven until crisp and tender, about 20 minutes. Brussels sprouts are delicious served with mustard sauce or lemon juice.

Buckwheat

Despite its name, buckwheat is not a type of wheat nor is it a grain; it's the seed from an herb. Buckwheat is commonly found hulled and crushed as groats, roasted groats or kasha.

benefits

Buckwheat contains more protein than grains do, and its protein is more nutritionally complete, which makes it a particularly good base for meatless meals. It's a healthy source of fiber, which fills you up and helps even out your blood sugar levels. Additionally, studies have shown that a phytochemical found in buckwheat may be capable of lowering blood sugar.

nutrients per serving:

**Buckwheat, kasha
½ cup cooked**

Calories 77
Protein 3g
Total Fat 0.5g
Saturated Fat 0g
Cholesterol 0g
Carbohydrate 17g
Dietary Fiber 2g
Sodium 0mg
Potassium 70mg
Calcium 6mg
Iron 0.7mg
Magnesium 43mg
Folate 12mcg

selection and storage

You can buy buckwheat groats whole or cracked into coarse, medium or fine grinds or roasted as kasha. Very finely cracked, unroasted groats, or buckwheat grits, are sold as hot cereal. Buckwheat flour is available in light and dark, depending on the amount of hull; darker versions have more fiber and a stronger flavor. Keep buckwheat in a well-sealed container in the refrigerator or freezer. At room temperature, it is susceptible to turning rancid.

preparation and serving tips

Buckwheat has an intense, nutty flavor. You can substitute buckwheat groats or kasha in most recipes calling for rice or other whole grains. Cook groats or kasha like rice, following package instructions for the amount of water. Buckwheat may be more familiar to you than you think. It can be found as a traditional kasha soup in Jewish delis and also as soba noodles in popular Japanese dishes. Buckwheat is not recommended for use in baking.

Bulgur

This Middle Eastern staple consists of wheat kernels that have been steamed, dried and crushed. It's an inexpensive, low-fat source of protein, making it a wonderfully nutritious and economical addition to a diabetes meal plan.

nutrients per serving:

Bulgur
½ cup cooked

Calories 76
Protein 3g
Total Fat 0g
Saturated Fat 0g
Cholesterol 0mg
Carbohydrate 17g
Dietary Fiber 4g
Sodium 5mg
Potassium 60mg
Calcium 9mg
Iron 0.9mg
Folate 16mcg

benefits

Bulgur makes an ideal foundation for a diabetes-wise diet. Its low-fat, low-calorie profile and generous dose of fiber make it a superstar ingredient. Bulgur doesn't lose many nutrients during its minimal processing, remaining high in protein and minerals. It is an excellent stand-in for fatty, calorie-laden protein sources, including meats, making it an especially helpful menu addition for people with diabetes who need to lose weight.

selection and storage

Bulgur is available in three grinds—coarse, medium and fine. Coarse bulgur is used to make pilaf or stuffing. Medium-grind bulgur is used in cereals. The finest grind of bulgur is used in the popular Middle Eastern cold salad called tabbouleh. Store bulgur in a screw-top glass jar in the refrigerator; it will keep for months.

preparation and serving tips

Because bulgur is already partially cooked, little time is needed for preparation. Simply combine ½ cup of bulgur with 1 cup of liquid and simmer for 5 minutes; let stand for 10 minutes and fluff with a fork. Bulgur triples in volume. If you like your bulgur chewier, let it sit longer to absorb more water. Bulgur can be used in place of rice in most recipes. Bulgur lends its nutty flavor to whatever it is combined with, allowing you to use it in a variety of dishes.

shrimp and bulgur salad

- ¾ cup water
- 6 tablespoons uncooked bulgur
- 2 medium plum tomatoes, diced
- 1 small red bell pepper, diced
- 6 ounces cooked tiny shrimp
- ¼ cup crumbled fat-free feta cheese
- ¼ cup chopped green onions, green part only
- ⅛ teaspoon salt
- ⅛ teaspoon black pepper
- 2 tablespoons vegetable juice
- 2 teaspoons white wine vinegar
- 1 teaspoon olive oil

1. Bring water to a boil in small saucepan over medium-high heat. Add bulgur; stir. Reduce heat to low; cover and cook 5 minutes. Remove from heat. Let stand 10 minutes.

nutrients per serving:

Calories 131
Calories from Fat 13%
Protein 15g
Carbohydrate 15g
Fiber 4g
Total Fat 2g
Saturated Fat <1g

Cholesterol 83mg
Sodium 258mg

Dietary Exchanges:
Starch 1
Meat 1½

2. Combine tomatoes, bell pepper, shrimp, feta cheese, green onions, salt and black pepper in large bowl. Stir in bulgur.

3. Whisk vegetable juice, vinegar and oil in small bowl or cup. Pour over salad; toss gently.

Makes 4 servings

Butternut Squash

Sweet and buttery tasting, this satisfying and fiber-rich winter squash makes an excellent addition to a diabetic meal plan. Its tough shell allows for longer storage so that we can enjoy it well into the winter months.

benefits

The fiber in butternut squash provides a feeling of fullness and also slows the rise in blood sugar levels after a meal. Beta-carotene, the antioxidant form of vitamin A, gives butternut squash its deep orange-yellow color. This essential vitamin helps maintain eye health and promote healthy skin—both of which are of special concern to people with diabetes, who are at increased risk of certain eye diseases and skin ulcers.

selection and storage

Butternut squash is available year-round; its peak season is from early fall through winter. It has a bulbous end and a smooth outer shell that ranges from yellow to camel-colored. Choose squash that is firm and free of bruises, punctures or cuts. Uncooked, it does not need refrigeration and can be stored in a cool, dark place for several weeks.

preparation and serving tips

The simplest way to prepare butternut squash is to cut it in half and bake or microwave. Because the skin is tough, use caution and a sharp knife to cut the squash. To help soften butternut squash for easier cutting, microwave for 3 to 5 minutes. Then, cut it in half lengthwise, scoop out the seeds and proceed with cooking or peeling. Add cubed squash to soups or stews. Or simply mash it and season with cinnamon or garlic and Parmesan cheese.

nutrients per serving:

**Butternut Squash
½ cup cooked**

Calories 41
Protein 1g
Total Fat 0g
Saturated Fat 0g
Cholesterol 0mg
Carbohydrate 11g

Dietary Fiber 3.5g
Sodium 0mg
Potassium 290mg
Calcium 42mg
Iron 0.6mg
Vitamin A 11,434 IU
Vitamin C 16mg
Folate 19mcg

roasted butternut squash

Nonstick cooking spray
1 pound butternut squash, peeled and cut
    into 1-inch cubes (about 4 cups)
2 medium onions, coarsely chopped
8 ounces carrots, peeled and cut into
    ½-inch diagonal slices (about 2 cups)
1 tablespoon dark brown sugar
¼ teaspoon salt
    Black pepper (optional)
1 tablespoon butter, melted

1. Preheat oven to 400°F. Line large baking sheet with foil and spray with cooking spray.

2. Arrange butternut squash, onions and carrots in single layer on prepared baking sheet; spray with cooking spray. Sprinkle with brown sugar, salt and pepper, if desired.

3. Bake 30 minutes. Stir gently; bake 10 to 15 minutes or until vegetables are tender. Drizzle with butter; toss to coat.

Makes 5 servings

nutrients per serving:

Calories 143
Calories from Fat 16%
Protein 3g
Carbohydrate 30g
Fiber 8g
Total Fat 3g
Saturated Fat 2g
Cholesterol 7mg
Sodium 167mg

Dietary Exchanges:
Vegetable 1
Starch 1½
Fat ½

Cabbage

Whether eaten raw or cooked, cabbage's versatility allows it to easily become a part of any meal. Making it even more appealing are its low calorie and fat contents.

benefits

Researchers have found that eating leafy green vegetables, such as cabbage, may reduce the risk of developing type 2 diabetes. For those who already have diabetes, cabbage offers fiber to help slow blood sugar's rise during a meal. Bok choy cabbage is an important nondairy source of calcium, which helps to prevent osteoporosis and control blood pressure. Savoy and bok choy cabbages provide beta-carotene, which reduces risks of heart disease and cancer.

selection and storage

There are hundreds of varieties of cabbage. When choosing green or red cabbage, pick a tight, compact head that looks crisp and fresh, with few loose leaves. Leafy varieties should be green, with firm stems. Store whole heads of cabbage in the crisper drawer of your refrigerator. Compact heads keep for a couple of weeks; leafy varieties, just a few days.

preparation and serving tips

Discard loose or limp outer leaves. To preserve nutrients and minimize cabbage's notorious odor during cooking, steam or stir-fry (in a nonaluminum pan) until slightly tender but still crisp, about 10 minutes for wedges, 5 minutes for shredded. Combine red and green cabbage for a colorful coleslaw, keeping calories down by using a dressing of nonfat yogurt. Bok choy and napa cabbage work well in stir-fry dishes, while savoy is perfect for stuffing. In place of the meat in stuffed cabbage recipes, use a fiber-filled substitute like bulgur, quinoa or buckwheat.

nutrients per serving:

Cabbage
½ cup cooked

Calories 17
Protein 1g
Total Fat 0g
Saturated Fat 0g
Cholesterol 0mg
Carbohydrate 4g
Dietary Fiber 1.5g
Sodium 6mg
Potassium 150mg
Calcium 36mg
Iron 0.1mg
Vitamin A 60 IU
Vitamin C 28mg
Folate 22mcg

lime-ginger coleslaw

    2 cups shredded green cabbage
1½ cups matchstick-size carrots
    1 cup shredded red cabbage
    ¼ cup finely chopped green onions
    3 tablespoons lime juice
    2 tablespoons sugar substitute or sugar
    2 tablespoons chopped fresh cilantro
    2 teaspoons vegetable or canola oil
1½ teaspoons grated fresh ginger
    ⅛ teaspoon salt
    ⅛ teaspoon red pepper flakes

Combine all ingredients in large bowl; toss well. Let stand 10 minutes before serving.

Makes 4 servings

nutrients per serving:

Calories 58
Calories from Fat 7%
Protein 2g
Carbohydrate 10g
Fiber 2g
Total Fat 2g
Saturated Fat 1g
Cholesterol 0mg
Sodium 106mg

Dietary Exchanges:
Vegetable 2

Carrots

Carrots are great for those watching what they eat. When eaten before a meal, their fiber helps fill you up so there's little room left for higher-calorie and carbohydrate foods.

benefits

Carrots' substantial fiber and otherwise low carbohydrate contents combined with their high vitamin A content make these popular vegetables a super food. Carrots' soluble fiber provides a feeling of fullness without adding calories and helps lower blood cholesterol levels, which are often elevated in people with diabetes. And when it comes to beta-carotene, carrots have few rivals; a mere ½ cup packs a huge amount of this antioxidant form of vitamin A. Beta-carotene helps defend the body's cells from damage, including cells in the heart, blood vessels and eyes, all of which are more vulnerable due to diabetes.

selection and storage

Look for firm carrots with bright orange color and smooth skin. Avoid carrots if they are limp or black near the top. Choose medium-sized ones that taper at the end; thicker ones may be tough. Baby-cut carrots are sweet and convenient. All carrots will keep for a few weeks.

preparation and serving tips

Wash and scrub whole carrots to remove soil contaminants. To remove pesticide residues, peel the outer layer and cut off the fat end. Carrots are a great raw snack, but their true sweet flavor shines through when cooked. Very little nutritional value is lost in cooking. Cooked carrots can be used in soups, sauces, casseroles and quick breads.

nutrients per serving:

Carrots
½ cup raw

Calories 25
Protein 1g
Total Fat 0g
Saturated Fat 0g
Cholesterol 0mg
Carbohydrate 6g
Dietary Fiber 2g
Sodium 40mg
Potassium 195mg
Calcium 20mg
Iron 0.2mg
Vitamin A 10,191 IU
Vitamin C 4mg
Folate 12mcg

chutney glazed carrots

2 cups cut peeled carrots (1½-inch pieces)
3 tablespoons cranberry or mango chutney
1 tablespoon Dijon mustard
2 teaspoons butter
2 tablespoons chopped pecans, toasted*

*Toast pecans in small skillet over medium heat 3 to 5 minutes or until fragrant, stirring frequently.

1. Place carrots in medium saucepan; add enough water to cover. Bring to a boil over high heat. Reduce heat; simmer 6 to 8 minutes or until carrots are tender.

2. Drain carrots; return to pan. Add chutney, mustard and butter. Cook and stir over medium heat 2 minutes or until carrots are glazed. Top with pecans just before serving.

Makes 4 servings

Cashews

This delicately flavored nut is a wise nut choice for people with diabetes. Researchers are studying the potential role of cashew-nut extract in the treatment of the disease.

nutrients per serving:

Cashews, dry roasted without salt
1 ounce

Calories 163
Protein 4g
Total Fat 13g
Saturated Fat 2.5g
Cholesterol 0mg
Carbohydrate 9g
Dietary Fiber 1g
Sodium 5mg
Potassium 160mg
Iron 1.7mg
Folate 20mcg
Vitamin E 0.3mg
Magnesium 74mg

benefits

Cashews have long been used in traditional medicine to treat high blood sugar, and recent research suggests an extract of the nut may improve the body's ability to respond to insulin and pull sugar from the blood. Cashews are also rich in magnesium, a mineral that has been associated with insulin resistance when it is lacking in the diet. Magnesium has also been found to assist in blood pressure control and other functions that help decrease risks of heart disease, stroke and diabetes. Cashews are lower in fat than many other popular nuts and contain little saturated fat. The fat they do contain is primarily monounsaturated oleic acid, the same fat in olive oil, which is considered heart healthy. Like other nuts, cashews provide protein and fiber, making them filling and satisfying.

selection and storage

Cashews are available oil roasted and salted but are most nutritious in their dry roasted and unsalted form. Because of their fat content, they should be stored in an airtight container in the refrigerator to prevent rancidity. Always check the "sell by" date on packages of cashews to be sure they are fresh.

preparation and serving tips

Cashews make wonderful nut butters and a tasty addition to salads and stir-fry dishes. As with most nuts, toasting cashews in the oven or on the stove top intensifies their flavor so you can use less of them in recipes (for less fat and calories). Enjoy cashews as a snack, but be sure to watch your portions.

Cauliflower

Despite its colorless appearance, cauliflower is more nutritious than you would believe. Filling, high in fiber and low in calories, it is an ideal vegetable for those with diabetes.

benefits

Cauliflower is low in sugars and starches, so it won't cause blood sugar to spike. Its healthy profile makes it a menu must for the many people with diabetes who need to lose excess weight. It's light in calories, and its extra crunchiness when served raw means it takes longer to chew, giving your body time to realize you're full before you overeat. Cauliflower is also a good source of vitamin C, folate and potassium.

selection and storage

Look for creamy white heads with compact florets; brown patches and opened florets are signs of aging. Store unwashed, uncut cauliflower loosely wrapped in a plastic bag in your refrigerator's crisper drawer for up to five days.

preparation and serving tips

Remove outer leaves, trim brown spots, break off florets and wash under cool running water before using. Cauliflower serves up well both raw and cooked. Raw, its flavor is less intense and great with a low-fat dip. Steam, bake, sauté or microwave cauliflower, but don't overcook it; overcooking destroys its vitamin C and folate contents and produces a bitter, pungent flavor. Although cheese sauces are popular, they add a hefty dose of fat and calories. Serve cauliflower plain or with a little fresh dill or olive oil. For a low-calorie substitute for mashed potatoes, mash cooked cauliflower with olive oil, garlic and milk.

nutrients per serving:

Cauliflower
½ cup cooked

Calories 14
Protein 1g
Total Fat 0g
Saturated Fat 0g
Cholesterol 0mg
Carbohydrate 3g
Dietary Fiber 1.5g
Sodium 10mg
Potassium 90mg
Calcium 10mg
Iron 0.2mg
Vitamin C 28mg
Folate 27mcg

Celery

Celery is a stereotypical diet food. Some people even believe that celery has "negative calories"—that you burn more calories from chewing it than the celery itself provides. While this is not true, in small portions, celery can be considered a "free food" for people with diabetes.

nutrients per serving:

Celery
½ cup raw

Calories 8
Protein 0g
Total Fat 0g
Saturated Fat 0g
Cholesterol 0mg
Carbohydrate 2g
Dietary Fiber 1g
Sodium 40mg
Potassium 130mg
Calcium 20mg
Iron 0.1mg
Vitamin A 227 IU
Vitamin C 2mg
Folate 18mcg

benefits

Celery is about 95 percent water by weight, so it's very low in calories, yet its fiber and crunchy texture make it both filling and satisfying to munch on. For people with diabetes who are trying to lose weight, it can be a healthy, helpful snack or salad addition. The celery leaves are actually the most nutritious part of the plant, containing more calcium, iron, potassium, beta-carotene and vitamin C than the stalks.

selection and storage

Choose firm bunches of celery that are tightly formed; the leaves should be green and crisp. Store celery in a plastic bag in the refrigerator up to two weeks, leaving the ribs attached to the stalk until ready to use.

preparation and serving tips

Separate celery stalks, rinse well to remove dirt from the inner stalk and remove the leaves. When serving celery raw, you can use a peeler to remove the outer threads. Pair raw celery with a low-fat dip or fill the stalk with protein-packed peanut butter or cream cheese for a hunger-fighting snack. When celery is sautéed with onions, it can add tons of flavor to soups, stews and casseroles. You can also try adding the nutrient-filled leaves to any dish.

moroccan lentil & vegetable soup

- 1 tablespoon olive oil
- 1 cup chopped onion
- 4 cloves garlic, minced
- ½ cup dried lentils, rinsed and sorted
- 1½ teaspoons ground coriander
- 1½ teaspoons ground cumin
- ½ teaspoon black pepper
- ½ teaspoon ground cinnamon
- 3¾ cups fat-free reduced-sodium chicken or vegetable broth
- ½ cup chopped celery
- ½ cup chopped sun-dried tomatoes (not packed in oil)
- 1 yellow squash, chopped
- ½ cup chopped green bell pepper
- 1 cup chopped plum tomatoes
- ½ cup chopped fresh Italian parsley
- ¼ cup chopped fresh cilantro or basil

1. Heat oil in medium saucepan over medium-high heat. Add onion and garlic; cook and stir 4 minutes or until onion is tender. Stir in lentils, coriander, cumin, black pepper and cinnamon; cook 2 minutes.

2. Add broth, celery and sun-dried tomatoes; bring to a boil. Reduce heat to medium-low; cover and simmer 25 minutes.

3. Stir in squash and bell pepper. Cover and cook 10 minutes or until lentils are tender.

4. Top with plum tomatoes, parsley and cilantro just before serving.

Makes 6 servings

Tip: Many soups taste best the next day, after the flavors have had time to blend. Cover and refrigerate the soup overnight, reserving the plum tomatoes, parsley and cilantro until ready to serve.

nutrients per serving:

Calories 131
Calories from Fat 20%
Protein 8g
Carbohydrate 20g
Fiber 2g
Total Fat 3g
Saturated Fat <1g
Cholesterol 0mg
Sodium 264mg

Dietary Exchanges:
Vegetable 1
Starch 1
Fat ½

Cheese

Any way you slice or shred it, cheese adds creaminess and a rich flavor to foods. When eaten in reasonable amounts, cheese livens up dishes. Despite its high-fat content, small amounts of cheese can be included in a diabetic meal plan.

benefits

Cheese is low in carbohydrates and therefore has very little effect on blood sugar levels. Its protein makes it a long-lasting energy source, but because it can be high in fat, it's a food to enjoy in moderation (serving size is about 1 ounce). Cheese is a concentrated source of many of the nutrients that are found in milk, including calcium, protein, phosphorus, potassium, vitamin A and vitamin B_{12}. Cheese has also been found to help protect teeth from cavity-causing bacteria.

selection and storage

There are hundreds of varieties of cheese, many available in various flavors and forms (sliced, cubed, shredded, grated, spreadable, etc.). Choose reduced-fat or part-skim varieties for fewer calories and less fat.

Purchase cheese by the "sell by" date and store it, tightly wrapped, in the refrigerator's cheese compartment for up to several weeks.

preparation and serving tips

Cheese can be eaten alone or added to other dishes. A little cheese pairs well with fruits, vegetables and grains, making these foods even more delicious. Full-flavored hard cheeses, such as Parmesan or Asiago, and aromatic sharp cheeses, such as Cheddar or Gorgonzola, can be used in smaller amounts to add intense flavor to dishes without a ton of excess calories.

nutrients per serving:

**Cheese, Cheddar
1 ounce**

Calories 114
Protein 7g
Total Fat 9g
Saturated Fat 6g
Cholesterol 30mg
Carbohydrate 0.5g
Dietary Fiber 0g
Sodium 176mg
Potassium 28mg
Calcium 204mg
Iron 0.2mg
Vitamin A 284 IU
Phosphorus 145mg
Vitamin B_{12} 0.3mcg

**Cheese, reduced-fat provolone
1 ounce**

Calories 77
Protein 7g
Total Fat 5g
Saturated Fat 3g
Cholesterol 15mg
Carbohydrate 1g
Dietary Fiber 0g
Sodium 245mg
Potassium 39mg
Calcium 212mg
Iron 0.2mg
Vitamin A 149 IU
Phosphorus 139mg
Vitamin B_{12} 0.4mcg

ham & egg breakfast panini

Nonstick cooking spray
¼ cup chopped green or red
    bell pepper
2 tablespoons sliced green onion
1 slice (1 ounce) reduced-fat
    smoked deli ham, chopped
    (about ¼ cup)
½ cup cholesterol-free egg
    substitute
Black pepper
4 slices multigrain or whole grain
    bread
2 slices (¾ ounce each) reduced-
    fat Cheddar or Swiss cheese

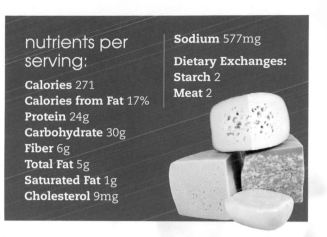

nutrients per serving:

Calories 271
Calories from Fat 17%
Protein 24g
Carbohydrate 30g
Fiber 6g
Total Fat 5g
Saturated Fat 1g
Cholesterol 9mg
Sodium 577mg

Dietary Exchanges:
Starch 2
Meat 2

1. Spray small skillet with cooking spray; heat over medium heat. Add bell pepper and green onion; cook and stir 4 minutes or until vegetables begin to soften. Stir in ham.

2. Combine egg substitute and black pepper in small bowl; pour into skillet. Cook about 2 minutes, stirring occasionally, until egg mixture is almost set.

3. Heat grill pan or medium skillet over medium heat. Spray one side of each bread slice with cooking spray; turn bread over. Top each of two bread slices with one cheese slice and half of egg mixture. Top with remaining bread slices.

4. Grill sandwiches, pressing lightly with spatula, about 2 minutes per side or until toasted. (If desired, cover pan with lid during last 2 minutes of cooking to melt cheese.) Cut sandwiches in half to serve.

Makes 2 servings

Chicken Breast

Chicken breast is a staple in any diet, as it is one of the leanest meats. It's a versatile source of high quality protein with significantly less saturated fat than other types of meats.

benefits

Of the edible parts of a chicken, the breast has the least fat. Removing the skin subtracts another 4 grams of fat (1 gram of it saturated, or "bad" fat) and roughly 60 calories. Chicken is also a good source of several B vitamins, including vitamins B_6, B_{12} and niacin, which are important for healthy immune function.

selection and storage

Chicken breasts are available in various forms; whole breasts with the skin on are the most economical. For convenience, boneless, skinless chicken breasts are available; just be aware of preseasoned chicken breasts that are higher in sodium. Refrigerate raw chicken for up to two days, cooked chicken up to three days. When freezing raw chicken, seal tightly in a plastic bag to prevent freezer burn. Use frozen chicken within two months.

preparation and serving tips

To keep chicken breast lean, use a low-fat cooking method such as baking, roasting, grilling, broiling or stewing. It makes little difference whether the skin is removed before or after cooking, but the meat is more moist and tender when cooked with the skin on. Cook chicken until the internal temperature is 165°F. Boneless chicken will cook faster than its bone-in counterpart, just avoid overcooking, which will make it dry and tough.

nutrients per serving:

Chicken Breast, skinless 3 ounces roasted

Calories 140
Protein 26g
Total Fat 3g
Saturated Fat 1g
Cholesterol 72mg
Carbohydrate 0g
Dietary Fiber 0g
Sodium 60mg
Potassium 220mg
Iron 0.9mg
Vitamin B_6 0.5mg
Vitamin B_{12} 0.3mcg
Niacin 12mcg

greek lemon chicken

4 boneless skinless chicken
   breasts (about ¼ pound each)
1 teaspoon grated lemon peel
2 tablespoons lemon juice
2 teaspoons extra virgin olive oil
1 teaspoon dried oregano
1 clove garlic, minced
¼ teaspoon salt
⅛ teaspoon black pepper
   Nonstick cooking spray
1 lemon, cut into wedges (optional)

nutrients per serving:

Calories 132
Calories from Fat 11%
Protein 27g
Carbohydrate 3g
Fiber 1g

Total Fat 2g
Saturated Fat <1g
Cholesterol 66mg
Sodium 74mg

Dietary Exchanges:
Meat 4

1. Place chicken in large resealable food storage bag. Add lemon peel, lemon juice, oil, oregano, garlic, salt and pepper. Seal bag; shake to coat chicken. Marinate in refrigerator at least 30 minutes or up to 8 hours.

2. Spray large nonstick skillet with cooking spray; heat over medium heat. Add chicken; cook 3 minutes. Turn over; reduce heat to medium-low. Cook 7 minutes or until no longer pink in center. Serve with lemon wedges, if desired.

Makes 4 servings

Chile Peppers

Ranging from mild to very hot, chile peppers add tons of spice and flavor to many dishes. Emerging research suggests these little packages also pack a powerful punch for health, including helping to lower blood glucose levels.

benefits

Early research suggests capsaicin, the substance that gives chile peppers their characteristic bite, may help improve insulin's effectiveness in lowering blood sugar after meals. These findings, if confirmed, could prove valuable for both the prevention and treatment of type 2 diabetes. Chile peppers are also rich in beta-carotene and vitamin C, important antioxidant warriors in the fight against heart disease, which is more common among people with diabetes.

selection and storage

Choose chile peppers based on the heat they provide. Mild to moderately hot peppers include Anaheim, ancho and poblano peppers, while hotter varieties include cayenne, jalapeño, serrano and habanero. Fresh chile peppers should have a deep, vivid color with no shriveling and should be stored in the vegetable drawer of the refrigerator. Chile peppers are available as chile pastes and hot sauces, and they can be dried to produce flakes and powders.

preparation and serving tips

To cool the fire of hot peppers, cut away the inside white membrane and discard the seeds. Wash hands, utensils and cutting board with soap and water after handling them and use gloves to prevent the oils from irritating your hands. Avoid touching your eyes while handling peppers. Chile peppers can be used in many types of dishes, especially in southwestern cooking. Dried chile flakes are an easy way to add spice to pizzas, salads, soups and chilis.

nutrients per serving:

Chile Peppers, red 2 tablespoons raw chopped

Calories 8
Protein 0g
Total Fat 0g
Saturated Fat 0g
Cholesterol 0mg
Carbohydrate 2g
Dietary Fiber <1g
Sodium 0mg
Potassium 60mg
Calcium 3mg
Iron 0.2mg
Vitamin A 178 IU
Vitamin C 27mg
Folate 4mcg

southern border meat loaf

1 pound 95% lean ground beef
1 can (8 ounces) tomato sauce, divided
½ cup finely chopped yellow onion
½ cup cornmeal
1 can (4 ounces) chopped mild green chiles
¼ cup chopped fresh cilantro
2 egg whites *or* 1 egg
1½ teaspoons ground cumin
¼ teaspoon salt
¼ teaspoon black pepper
2 tablespoons ketchup

1. Preheat oven to 350°F. Spray baking sheet with nonstick cooking spray.

2. Combine beef, half of tomato sauce, onion, cornmeal, chiles, cilantro, egg whites, cumin, salt and pepper in large bowl; mix well. Combine remaining tomato sauce and ketchup in small bowl.

3. Place meat mixture on prepared baking sheet; shape into 6×9-inch oval. Top with tomato sauce mixture. Bake 55 minutes or until cooked through (160°F). Let stand 5 minutes before slicing. *Makes 4 servings*

nutrients per serving:

Calories 248
Calories from Fat 22%
Protein 27g
Carbohydrate 22g
Fiber 3g
Total Fat 6g
Saturated Fat 2g
Cholesterol 59mg
Sodium 684mg

Dietary Exchanges:
Starch 1½
Meat 3

Cinnamon

Used for centuries as a culinary spice and for medicinal purposes, cinnamon is now gaining attention as an aid for regulating blood sugar levels.

benefits

Several studies have shown improved insulin sensitivity and blood glucose control from consuming as little as ½ teaspoon of cinnamon per day. Cinnamon may also help lower blood cholesterol and triglyceride levels, which are often elevated in people with type 2 diabetes. Cinnamon contains more protective antioxidants than most other spices and many foods do. You'll find as many antioxidants in 1 teaspoon of cinnamon as in a full cup of pomegranate juice or ½ cup of blueberries. Cinnamon is also a good source of chromium, an essential mineral that enhances the action of insulin.

selection and storage

Cinnamon is available ground or as sticks, or scrolls, of dried bark. Ground cinnamon has a stronger flavor than the sticks and can stay fresh for six months, while the scrolls last longer. Both should be stored in a cool, dark, dry place.

preparation and serving tips

Cinnamon adds a warm, distinctive flavor to both sweet and savory dishes. It is often paired with apples and added to sweet baked goods, but it also adds a pungent flavor to Middle Eastern and Asian dishes, especially as an ingredient in curry powder. Be adventurous with cinnamon—the possibilities are endless. Perk up drinks such as coffee, tea, smoothies or mulled wine with ground cinnamon or sticks of cinnamon. Sprinkle cinnamon on cereal, ice cream, pudding or yogurt. Spice up your meats by adding cinnamon to marinades for lamb or beef.

nutrients per serving:

**Cinnamon, ground
1 teaspoon**

Calories 6
Protein 0g
Total Fat 0g
Saturated Fat 0g
Cholesterol 0mg
Carbohydrate 2g
Dietary Fiber 1g
Sodium 0mg
Potassium 11mg
Calcium 26mg
Iron 0.2mg
Vitamin A 8 IU

no-bake pumpkin mousse parfaits

2 ounces reduced-fat cream cheese, softened
1 can (15 ounces) solid-pack pumpkin
¾ cup fat-free (skim) milk
1 package (4-serving size) vanilla fat-free sugar-free instant pudding and pie filling mix
1 teaspoon ground cinnamon
½ teaspoon ground ginger
⅛ teaspoon ground cloves
3 cups thawed reduced-fat whipped topping, divided
4 gingersnap cookies, crushed

1. Beat cream cheese in medium bowl with electric mixer at medium speed until smooth. Add pumpkin, milk, pudding mix, cinnamon, ginger and cloves; beat 1 minute or until smooth. Fold in 1½ cups whipped topping.

2. Spoon ¼ cup mousse into each of eight 6-ounce dessert glasses. Spoon 2 tablespoons whipped topping over each dessert. Top with ¼ cup mousse. Cover and refrigerate 1 hour.

3. Top each parfait with remaining whipped topping and crushed gingersnaps just before serving. *Makes 8 servings*

nutrients per serving:

Calories 138
Calories from Fat 39%
Protein 3g
Carbohydrate 19g
Fiber 2g
Total Fat 6g
Saturated Fat 3g
Cholesterol 5mg
Sodium 249mg

Dietary Exchanges:
Starch 1
Fat 1

Coffee

Best loved for the caffeine buzz it provides, emerging research suggests that coffee may offer a protection against type 2 diabetes, an even greater reason to down this popular beverage.

benefits

A promising, but so far unexplained, scientific observation is that coffee drinkers are less likely to develop diabetes. But even for those who already have the disease, coffee may offer benefits. Both regular and decaf coffee contain minerals, such as chromium and magnesium, that help the body use insulin. Coffee is rich in antioxidants, which help protect the vulnerable heart and blood vessels of a person with diabetes. Plus, plain black coffee is a great choice for anyone who is diet-conscious, as it is essentially calorie free.

selection and storage

You'll find several coffee selections at the store—from whole to ground, mild- to full-bodied, caffeinated or decaffeinated to instant and flavored. Choose the form and flavor depending on your preparation and your taste preferences. Store coffee beans or ground coffee in an airtight container in a cool, dry place. Whole beans should be used within a week. Ground coffee should be used within a few days. For long-term storage, keep coffee in the freezer.

preparation and serving tips

The calorie-free beverage we should indulge in isn't always what we choose. Beware of coffee drinks loaded with sugary syrups, whole milk and whipped cream, which can add loads of calories and fat. Coffee is a wonderful flavor enhancer and adds depth to various recipes, from desserts to main dishes, including chilis, pasta sauces and marinades or glazes for meats.

nutrients per serving:

Coffee
1 cup brewed

Calories 2
Protein 0g
Total Fat 0g

Saturated Fat 0g
Cholesterol 0mg
Carbohydrate 0g
Dietary Fiber 0g
Sodium 5mg

Potassium 116mg
Magnesium 7mg
Calcium 5mg
Folate 5mcg

coffee granita

2 cups water
¼ cup powdered sugar
2 tablespoons sucralose-based sugar
   substitute
1½ tablespoons instant coffee granules

1. Combine water, powdered sugar, sugar substitute and coffee granules in small saucepan. Bring to a boil over medium-high heat, stirring until completely dissolved.

2. Pour into 8-inch square baking pan; cover with foil. Freeze 2 hours or until slushy. Stir to break into small chunks. Cover and freeze 2 hours. Stir to break up again. Cover and freeze at least 4 hours or overnight.

3. Scrape surface with large metal spoon. Spoon into individual bowls. Serve immediately. *Makes 5 servings*

nutrients per serving:

Calories 30
Calories from Fat 0%
Protein 0g
Carbohydrate 7g
Fiber 0g
Total Fat 0g
Saturated Fat 0g
Cholesterol 0mg
Sodium 0mg

Dietary Exchanges:
Starch ½

Cottage Cheese

Cottage cheese has gotten a bad rap as a standard diet food, but it has many uses besides a boring breakfast. It makes a great nutritious swap for the unhealthy ingredients found in many favorite dishes.

benefits

Cottage cheese is considered a dairy option in a traditional diabetic meal plan, but it's lower in carbohydrates and higher in protein than milk and yogurt. It provides long-lasting energy with little effect on blood sugar levels. Plus, it makes a great meat alternative, as the protein in cottage cheese is high quality. Select a fat-free or low-fat version, and this dieting staple can help you feel satisfied on fewer calories and less fat, which is good news for those who need to lose weight.

selection and storage

Choose low-fat (1%) or fat-free cottage cheese for less calories and fat than whole milk (4%) cottage cheese. It comes in small, medium or large curd, which does not affect its nutrition profile. You can buy cottage cheese flavored, such as with chives or pineapple. Cottage cheese is perishable and must be stored in the refrigerator.

preparation and serving tips

The flavor of cottage cheese goes well with fresh vegetables, such as tomatoes and bell peppers, and with fruits, such as pineapple and berries. Low-fat or fat-free cottage cheese makes a useful ingredient in various recipes. Use it to replace higher-fat cream cheese in desserts like cheesecakes and in dips. It also works great in place of high-fat cheeses in pasta dishes, such as lasagna or stuffed shells, and in egg-based dishes, such as quiches or frittatas.

nutrients per serving:

Cottage Cheese, low-fat (1%) ½ cup

Calories 81
Protein 14g
Total Fat 1g
Saturated Fat 0.5g
Cholesterol 5mg
Carbohydrate 3g
Dietary Fiber 0g
Sodium 460mg
Potassium 95mg
Calcium 69mg
Vitamin A 46 IU
Folate 14mcg

roasted pepper and sourdough brunch casserole

- 3 cups sourdough bread cubes
- 1 jar (12 ounces) roasted red pepper strips, drained
- 1 cup (4 ounces) shredded reduced-fat sharp Cheddar cheese
- 1 cup (4 ounces) shredded reduced-fat Monterey Jack cheese
- 1 cup fat-free cottage cheese
- 1½ cups cholesterol-free egg substitute
- 1 cup fat-free (skim) milk
- ¼ cup chopped fresh cilantro
- ¼ teaspoon black pepper

1. Spray 11×7-inch baking dish with nonstick cooking spray. Place bread cubes in baking dish. Arrange roasted peppers evenly over bread cubes; sprinkle with Cheddar and Monterey Jack cheeses.

2. Place cottage cheese in food processor or blender; process until smooth. Add egg substitute and milk; process just until blended. Pour over ingredients in baking dish. Sprinkle with cilantro and black pepper. Cover; refrigerate 4 to 12 hours or overnight.

3. Preheat oven to 375°F. Bake 40 minutes or until center is set and top is golden brown.

Makes 8 servings

nutrients per serving:

Calories 179
Calories from Fat 28%
Protein 19g
Carbohydrate 13g
Fiber 1g

Total Fat 6g
Saturated Fat 3g
Cholesterol 22mg
Sodium 704mg

Dietary Exchanges:
Starch 1
Meat 2

Cucumber

Cucumber is an incredibly light and refreshing food to enjoy, with green skin, mild and crisp flesh and tender seeds. Whether eaten alone or added to sandwiches or salads, this low-calorie, filling food is a wonderful choice for those with diabetes.

benefits

Because cucumbers are approximately 95 percent water, they are very low in calories. With such high water and low carbohydrate contents, cucumbers add low-calorie bulk and satisfying crunch to meals without having much effect on blood sugar levels.

selection and storage

Cucumbers are available year-round. Choose firm cucumbers with smooth, brightly colored skins. If you plan to eat the seeds, avoid larger cucumbers— as the fruit matures, the seeds grow larger and develop a bitter taste. Smaller cucumbers are used to make pickles. Store unwashed cucumbers, in a plastic bag, in the refrigerator for up to ten days. Cut cucumbers can be refrigerated, tightly wrapped, for up to five days.

preparation and serving tips

Wash cucumbers thoroughly just before using. Supermarket cucumbers are covered with an edible wax to protect them from moisture loss. If you prefer not to eat the wax you can peel the cucumber or use a produce rinse. Cucumbers can be eaten in a multitude of ways. Serve cucumber slices as a refreshing snack with a low-fat dip or add them to salads for a delightful crunch. Try an Indian-inspired salad with cucumbers, fresh herbs and plain yogurt. Cucumber makes an excellent main ingredient in a light, low-calorie cold soup. Be adventurous—pickle your own cucumbers for a crisp and refreshing garnish.

nutrients per serving:

Cucumber
½ cup raw

Calories 8
Protein 0g
Total Fat 0g
Saturated Fat 0g
Cholesterol 0mg
Carbohydrate 2g
Dietary Fiber <1g
Sodium 0mg
Potassium 75mg
Calcium 8mg
Iron 0.2mg
Vitamin A 55 IU
Vitamin C 2mg
Folate 4mcg

tomato, avocado and cucumber salad with feta cheese

1½ tablespoons extra virgin olive oil
1 tablespoon balsamic vinegar
1 clove garlic, minced
¼ teaspoon salt
¼ teaspoon black pepper
2 cups diced seeded plum tomatoes
1 small ripe avocado, diced into
    ½-inch chunks
½ cup chopped cucumber
⅓ cup crumbled reduced-fat feta cheese
4 large red leaf lettuce leaves
    Chopped fresh basil (optional)

1. Whisk oil, vinegar, garlic, salt and pepper in medium bowl. Add tomatoes and avocado; toss lightly.

2. Stir in cucumber and feta cheese; spoon onto lettuce leaves. Top with basil, if desired.

Makes 4 servings

nutrients per serving:

Calories 138	**Saturated Fat** 2g
Calories from Fat 72%	**Cholesterol** 3mg
Protein 4g	**Sodium** 311mg
Carbohydrate 7g	**Dietary Exchanges:**
Fiber 2g	**Vegetable** 1½
Total Fat 11g	**Fat** 2

Dark Chocolate

Contrary to popular belief, people with diabetes can indulge in sweets. In fact, moderate amounts of dark chocolate can fit in your diabetes meal plan without sending your blood sugar soaring.

nutrients per serving:

**Dark Chocolate
1 ounce**

Calories 154
Protein 1g
Total Fat 9g
Saturated Fat 5g
Cholesterol 2mg
Carbohydrate 17g
Dietary Fiber 2g
Sodium 6mg
Potassium 160mg
Calcium 16mg
Iron 2.3mg
Magnesium 43mg
Copper 0.3mg
Phosphorus 60mg

benefits

Unlike other candies or sweet foods, dark chocolate has little effect on blood sugar. And it contains antioxidants, essential minerals and plant nutrients called flavanols that help protect the heart by lowering blood pressure and improving circulation. Shielding the heart from damage is particularly important for people with diabetes, since the disease increases the risk of cardiovascular disease. Still, moderation is essential, as dark chocolate is high in calories and saturated fat. To get the most benefit without overdoing calories, enjoy no more than 1 or 2 ounces per week.

selection and storage

Dark chocolate is available in varying levels of "darkness," depending on the percentage of cocoa. For example, 60 percent cocoa content means that 40 percent of the product is made up of sugar, vanilla and other ingredients. The higher the percentage of cocoa, the less sweet and more bitter it will taste. Dark chocolate includes semisweet and bittersweet varieties. Store dark chocolate tightly wrapped in a cool, dry place; warmer temperatures will cause grayish streaks and blotches, which do not affect flavor. Under ideal conditions, it can be stored for years without losing quality.

preparation and serving tips

Dark chocolate is a delicacy that is best enjoyed on its own. It can also be used in baking, in a wide variety of desserts or simply as a garnish for a low-calorie dessert.

Edamame

Edamame is the Japanese name for fresh green soybeans. Enjoyed straight from the pod or shelled and added to recipes, the beans of this tender legume hold promise for helping to improve the health of people with diabetes.

benefits

Edamame are low in calories and a rich source of both fiber and protein—nutrients that help you feel full longer and keep your blood sugar level on an even keel. Unlike most plant sources of protein, edamame provide a complete protein—one that includes all the amino acids required by the body. This soy protein is believed to help reduce insulin resistance and prevent kidney damage and liver disease in people with diabetes. Research also links soy foods to lower blood cholesterol levels.

selection and storage

Fresh edamame, in the pods or already shelled, may be available in ethnic markets in the produce section. Most often edamame can be found in the frozen vegetable section. Fresh edamame can be stored in the refrigerator for up to two weeks. Frozen packages can be stored up to six months.

preparation and serving tips

To cook edamame, boil, steam, sauté or microwave—either the whole pods or just the beans. You can eat edamame right out of the pods as a snack or appetizer. The pods are tough and should be discarded. The beans make a great alternative for those nights you want to go meatless. Add the beans to a variety of dishes, such as stews, salads, soups or pasta or rice dishes, for added fiber and protein.

nutrients per serving:

**Edamame, shelled
½ cup cooked**

Calories 95
Protein 8g
Total Fat 4g
Saturated Fat 0.5g
Cholesterol 0mg
Carbohydrate 8g
Dietary Fiber 4g
Sodium 5mg
Potassium 340mg
Calcium 49mg
Iron 1.7mg
Vitamin C 5mg
Folate 241mcg

Eggplant

Filling and low in calories, this versatile vegetable is part of many popular ethnic dishes, including Indian curries, Greek moussaka, Middle Eastern baba ghanoush and French ratatouille.

benefits

Eggplant is a decent source of fiber and potassium, but what makes it an especially appropriate addition to diabetic meal plans is that it's low in carbohydrates, so it doesn't cause spikes in blood sugar. It's also low in calories, so it can assist weight-loss efforts. Eggplant's meaty texture and flavor make it perfect for low-fat meatless dishes loaded with nutrient-rich grains, legumes and vegetables.

selection and storage

Choose eggplant that is small, firm and thin-skinned. Larger ones tend to be seedy, tough and bitter. The skin should range in color from deep purple to light violet or white. Eggplant is best used within a few days but may be refrigerated for up to a week.

preparation and serving tips

Eggplant can be eaten with or without the skin; use a potato peeler to remove the skin. To help reduce the bitterness, slice eggplant, sprinkle with salt and let it stand for 30 minutes. Then, drain and blot dry before cooking. Eggplant can be baked, roasted, grilled, steamed or sautéed. Eggplant is done when it can be pierced easily with a fork. It tends to absorb fats easily, so go easy on fatty ingredients to keep calories low. Eggplant makes a tasty addition to stir-fries and lasagna and pasta dishes. Or it can be stuffed with other flavorful veggies and baked.

nutrients per serving:

**Eggplant
½ cup cooked**

Calories 17
Protein 0g
Total Fat 0g
Saturated Fat 0g
Cholesterol 0mg
Carbohydrate 4g
Dietary Fiber 1g
Sodium 0mg
Potassium 60mg
Calcium 3mg
Iron 0.1mg
Vitamin A 18 IU
Vitamin C 1mg
Folate 7mcg

eggplant parmesan

Nonstick cooking spray

2 egg whites

2 tablespoons water

6 tablespoons Italian-seasoned dry bread crumbs

2 tablespoons grated Parmesan cheese

1 large eggplant, peeled and cut into 12 round slices

2 teaspoons olive oil

1 small onion, diced

1 clove garlic, minced

2 cans (about 14 ounces each) no-salt-added diced tomatoes

½ teaspoon dried basil

½ teaspoon dried oregano

2 ounces part-skim mozzarella cheese, shredded

1 ounce grated reduced-fat Parmesan cheese

1. Preheat oven to 350°F. Spray large baking pan with cooking spray.

2. Whisk egg whites and water in shallow dish. Combine bread crumbs and Parmesan cheese in separate shallow dish. Dip eggplant slices in egg white mixture, then in bread crumb mixture, pressing lightly to adhere crumbs.

nutrients per serving:

Calories 227

Calories from Fat 32%

Protein 12g

Carbohydrate 31g

Fiber 9g

Total Fat 8g

Saturated Fat 2g

Cholesterol 11mg

Sodium 610mg

Dietary Exchanges:

Starch 2

Meat 2

Fat ½

3. Place eggplant slices in single layer in prepared pan. Spray with cooking spray. Bake 25 to 30 minutes or until bottoms are browned. Turn slices; bake 10 to 15 minutes or until well browned.

4. Meanwhile, heat oil in medium nonstick skillet over medium-high heat. Add onion; cook and stir about 5 minutes or until translucent. Add garlic; cook and stir 1 minute. Stir in tomatoes, basil and oregano; bring to a boil. Reduce heat to low; simmer 15 to 20 minutes or until sauce is thickened, stirring occasionally.

5. Spray 13×9-inch baking dish with cooking spray. Spread sauce in dish. Arrange eggplant slices in single layer on top of sauce. Sprinkle with mozzarella and reduced-fat Parmesan cheeses. Bake 15 to 20 minutes or until sauce is bubbly and cheese is melted.

Makes 4 servings

Eggs

or years, eggs have been shed in a negative light. Yet the incredible egg is quite beneficial. Eating eggs is a great way to start your day, as they are rich in protein and many nutrients.

nutrients per serving:

Egg
1 large boiled

Calories 78
Protein 6g
Total Fat 5g
Saturated Fat 2g
Cholesterol 186mg
Carbohydrate <1g
Dietary Fiber 0g
Sodium 60mg
Potassium 65mg
Calcium 25mg
Iron 0.6mg
Vitamin A 260 IU
Vitamin D 44 IU
Choline 113mg

benefits

Even though eggs are high in cholesterol, research indicates they can be a healthy addition to a diabetes meal plan. Eggs offer 13 essential vitamins and minerals, high-quality protein, healthy unsaturated fats and protective antioxidants—all for about 75 calories per egg. Enjoying eggs at breakfast has been shown to help control both hunger and blood sugar levels. But what about all that cholesterol? It turns out the saturated fat in the foods we eat, far more than the cholesterol content, is what jacks up cholesterol levels. And eggs are actually rather low in saturated fats. But keep in mind, pairing eggs with bacon and sausage—foods loaded with saturated fat—will not favor your cholesterol levels.

selection and storage

Choose eggs that are clean and not cracked, and always check the "sell-by" date for freshness. Brown eggs and those labeled as "farm-laid" or "free-range" are no more nutritious. However, eggs from hens fed a diet rich in omega-3 fatty acids will contain more of this healthy fat. Store eggs in the carton in the main part of the refrigerator and use within three weeks.

preparation and serving tips

From scrambled eggs to egg soufflés, eggs are a versatile food on their own. They also serve as an essential ingredient in recipes—helping baked goods to rise, binding ingredients in casseroles, thickening custards and sauces and emulsifying mayonnaise and salad dressings, to name a few.

angelic deviled eggs

    6 eggs
    ¼ cup low-fat (1%) cottage cheese
    3 tablespoons fat-free ranch dressing
    2 teaspoons Dijon mustard
    2 tablespoons minced fresh chives or dill
    1 tablespoon diced well-drained pimiento
       or roasted red pepper

1. Place eggs in medium saucepan; add enough water to cover by 1 inch. Cover and bring to a boil over high heat. Remove from heat; let stand 15 minutes. Drain. Add enough cold water to cover eggs in saucepan; let stand until eggs are cool. Drain and peel.

2. Cut eggs in half lengthwise. Remove yolks, reserving three yolk halves. Discard remaining yolks or reserve for another use. Place egg whites, cut sides up, on large plate; cover with plastic wrap and refrigerate until ready to use.

3. Combine cottage cheese, dressing, musta and reserved yolk halves in food processor; process until smooth. (Or place in small bowl and mash with fork until well blended.) Transfer to small bowl; stir in chives and pimiento. Spoon into egg whites. Cover and refrigerate at least 1 hour.

Makes 12 servings

nutrients per serving:

Calories 44
Calories from Fat 52%
Protein 4g
Carbohydrate 1g
Fiber 1g
Total Fat 3g
Saturated Fat <1g
Cholesterol 27mg
Sodium 96mg

Dietary Exchanges:
Meat ½

Fennel

This vegetable may be a stranger to many, but it shouldn't be! Fennel provides wonderful flavor and texture to many dishes, as well as plenty of nutrients.

benefits

Fennel provides several essential nutrients without contributing much in the way of carbohydrates or calories, making it a good food to include in your diet if you have type 2 diabetes.

In addition to offering vitamin C, calcium, iron and folate, fennel is a good source of potassium and fiber, which is great for the many people with diabetes who also have heart disease. The potassium helps lower blood pressure and the fiber helps lower blood cholesterol. The fiber also prevents wild spikes in blood sugar levels.

selection and storage

Select fennel that has a whitish bulb, white to pale green stalks and light green and delicate leaves. The bulb should be firm and without signs of browning or drying. Store fennel in a plastic bag in the crisper drawer for up to five days. Fennel seeds are available both ground and whole in the spice section of the supermarket.

preparation and serving tips

All parts of fennel can be used—stalks, leaves and bulb. Rinse fennel well to remove dirt from the bulb and between the stalks. Fennel can be enjoyed in many ways: raw in salads, braised or sautéed as a side dish or in soups and stews. The fragrant greens can be used as a garnish and as a flavor enhancer. Fennel seeds are often added to meatballs or meat loaves for an Italian flavor.

nutrients per serving:

Fennel
½ cup raw

Calories 13
Protein 1g
Total Fat 0g
Saturated Fat 0g
Cholesterol 0mg
Carbohydrate 3g
Dietary Fiber 1g
Sodium 25mg
Potassium 180mg
Calcium 21mg
Iron 0.3mg
Vitamin A 58 IU
Vitamin C 5mg
Folate 12mcg

vegetable couscous

- 1 teaspoon olive oil
- ½ small bulb fennel, chopped
- ⅓ cup thinly sliced carrot
- ¼ cup chopped shallots or onion
- 1 clove garlic, minced
- ⅓ cup low-sodium vegetable juice
- ⅓ cup water
- ¼ teaspoon hot pepper sauce
- ⅛ teaspoon salt
- ⅓ cup uncooked whole wheat or regular couscous

1. Heat oil in medium saucepan over medium heat. Add fennel, carrot, shallots and garlic; cook 5 minutes, stirring occasionally. Add vegetable juice, water, hot pepper sauce and salt; bring to a simmer. Cover and simmer 5 to 6 minutes or until vegetables are tender.

2. Stir in couscous. Turn off heat; cover and let stand 5 minutes or until liquid is absorbed. Fluff with fork.

Makes 2 servings

nutrients per serving:

Calories 202
Calories from Fat 13%
Protein 7g
Carbohydrate 39g
Fiber 8g

Total Fat 3g
Saturated Fat <1g
Cholesterol 0mg
Sodium 212mg

Dietary Exchanges:
Starch 2½
Fat ½

Fish

Fish is a smart catch for any diet—its high protein and low saturated fat contents make it the perfect substitute for fattier meats.

benefits

Eating at least two servings of fish each week offers multiple health benefits of special value to people with diabetes, such as improving the body's handling of blood sugar and warding off diseases of the heart, kidneys and eyes—organs particularly vulnerable to damage from high blood sugar. The essential omega-3 fatty acids in the fish's oil deliver most of these benefits. Fish rich in omega-3 fats include salmon, mackerel, sardines, anchovies, trout, tuna, whitefish, bass, ocean perch and halibut.

selection and storage

Whether whole, fillets or steaks, fish should be firm and moist. Scales should be shiny and clean, not slimy. If you don't cook fresh fish the same day you buy it, store in the refrigerator for a day or wrap well and freeze. Frozen fish will keep up to six months.

preparation and serving tips

For leaner fish (most varieties with light-colored flesh), use moist-heat methods such as poaching, steaming or baking with vegetables. Dry-heat methods, such as baking, broiling and grilling, work well for fattier fish. Fish cooks quite fast; it's done when it looks opaque and the flesh just begins to flake. The rule of thumb is to bake for 8 to 10 minutes per inch of thickness, measured at the thickest point. For grilling or broiling, cook 4 to 5 minutes per inch of thickness.

nutrients per serving:

**Whitefish
3 ounces cooked**

Calories 146
Protein 21g
Total Fat 6g
Saturated Fat 1g
Cholesterol 65mg
Carbohydrate 0g
Dietary Fiber 0g
Sodium 55mg
Potassium 345mg
Phosphorus 294mg
Iron 0.4mg
Vitamin B$_{12}$ 0.8mcg
Selenium 14mcg

grilled tilapia with zesty mustard sauce

2 tablespoons light tub margarine
1 teaspoon Dijon mustard
½ teaspoon grated lemon peel
½ teaspoon low-sodium
    Worcestershire sauce
½ teaspoon salt, divided
¼ teaspoon black pepper
4 thin mild fish fillets, such as tilapia
    (about 4 ounces each)
1½ teaspoons paprika
    Nonstick cooking spray
½ medium lemon, quartered
2 tablespoons finely chopped fresh
    parsley

1. Prepare grill for direct cooking.

2. Whisk margarine, mustard, lemon peel, Worcestershire sauce, ¼ teaspoon salt and pepper in small bowl until well blended. Set aside.

3. Rinse fish and pat dry with paper towels. Sprinkle both sides of fish with paprika and remaining ¼ teaspoon salt. Lightly spray grill basket with cooking spray. Place fish in basket. Grill over medium-high heat, covered, 3 minutes. Turn and grill, covered, 2 to 3 minutes or until fish begins to flake when tested with fork.

4. Squeeze one lemon wedge over each fillet. Spoon mustard sauce over fish. Sprinkle with parsley.   *Makes 4 servings*

nutrients per serving:

Calories 136
Calories from Fat 30%
Protein 23g
Carbohydrate 1g
Fiber 1g
Total Fat 5g

Saturated Fat <1g
Cholesterol 57mg
Sodium 423mg

Dietary Exchanges:
Meat 3

Flax Seed

Many people had never heard of flax seed until recent years. Its popularity has increased immensely because of its powerful health benefits. To unlock its potential, flax seed must be ground before eating.

nutrients per serving:

**Flax Seed
1 tablespoon ground**

Calories 37
Protein 1g
Total Fat 3g
Saturated Fat 0g
Cholesterol 0mg
Carbohydrate 2g
Dietary Fiber 2g
Sodium 0mg
Potassium 60mg
Calcium 18mg
Iron 0.4mg
Phosphorus 45mg
Magnesium 27mg

benefits

Flax seed's nutrient profile makes it ideal for people with diabetes: It's high in fiber, which helps keep blood sugar levels steady, but very low in the other types of carbohydrates—the sugars and starches that cause blood sugar to shoot upwards. It also carries a substantial dose of omega-3 fatty acids, an essential polyunsaturated fat the body cannot make for itself. Recent research suggests omega-3 fats may improve insulin sensitivity and help prevent diabetic retinopathy, the leading cause of blindness that affects millions of people with the disease.

selection and storage

Flax seed is available whole or ground into meal. Because ground flax will go rancid quickly, it's better to buy whole flax seed and grind it yourself, which takes seconds in a food processor or blender. Once ground, flax seed should be stored in an airtight container in the freezer and used within a few weeks. Whole flax seed stays fresh for up to a year if stored in a cool, dark, dry place.

preparation and serving tips

Flax seed has a pleasant nutty flavor, but it's almost undetectable when added to many foods. A few tablespoons of ground flax seed can be added to baked goods, such as breads, muffins, cookies and pancakes. Sprinkle over cottage cheese, yogurt, cereal or salads. Add it to smoothies for a heart-healthy boost. It can also be cooked into meat loaves, meatballs and casseroles.

pm snack bars

- 3 tablespoons creamy peanut butter
- 2 tablespoons molasses
- 2 egg whites
- 2 tablespoons ground flax seed
- 4 cups crisp rice cereal
- ½ cup sliced almonds
- 1 ounce bittersweet chocolate, melted

1. Preheat oven to 350°F. Spray 9-inch square baking pan with nonstick cooking spray. Place peanut butter in small microwavable bowl; microwave on LOW (30%) 30 seconds or until melted. Stir in molasses; set aside.

2. Place egg whites and flax seed in blender; blend until foamy. Pour into large bowl. Add peanut butter mixture; stir until smooth. Stir in cereal and almonds until evenly coated. Press into prepared pan.

3. Bake 20 to 25 minutes or until lightly browned. Cool completely in pan on wire rack. Drizzle melted chocolate over bars.

Makes 16 servings

nutrients per serving:

Calories 91
Calories from Fat 41%
Protein 3g
Carbohydrate 11g
Fiber 1g
Total Fat 4g
Saturated Fat 1g
Cholesterol <1mg
Sodium 24mg

Dietary Exchanges:
Starch ½
Fat 1

Garlic

If you don't already love garlic's pungent taste, you should. Not only does it add a ton of flavor when used in cooking, it has wonderful health benefits, too.

benefits

Whenever garlic is crushed or cooked, a substance called allicin is formed, providing garlic's distinctive aroma and flavor. Allicin may also play a significant role in heart health, which is important for people with diabetes, who are at a higher risk for heart disease. Studies indicate garlic may help lower high blood pressure and slow the hardening of arteries that often lead to heart disease or stroke. Garlic also thins the blood, which may help prevent blood clots but also could cause problems during trauma or surgery; your best bet is to consult your doctor on this.

selection and storage

Pink-skinned garlic is sweeter and keeps longer than white garlic. Large elephant garlic is milder in flavor and can be used similarly to leeks. Choose loose garlic that is firm to the touch with no visible damp or brown spots. Store garlic in a cool, dark, dry spot; it will last anywhere from a few weeks to a few months. If garlic begins to sprout, just remove the tough, green sprout. Jarred garlic and garlic powder are convenient but not as flavorful as fresh. If using garlic salt, keep in mind it contains a lot of sodium.

preparation and serving tips

Use pressed garlic when you want full-force garlic flavor to come through and minced garlic when you want milder flavor. For a buttery flavor, bake whole cloves until tender. The longer garlic is cooked, the milder the flavor.

nutrients per serving:

Garlic 1 clove		
Calories 4	Saturated Fat 0g	Potassium 10mg
Protein 0g	Cholesterol 0mg	Calcium 5mg
Total Fat 0g	Carbohydrate 1g	Iron 0.1mg
	Dietary Fiber 0g	Vitamin C 1mg
	Sodium 0mg	

kale with lemon and garlic

   2 bunches kale or Swiss chard (1 to 1¼ pounds)
   1 tablespoon olive or vegetable oil
   3 cloves garlic, minced
   ½ cup reduced-sodium chicken broth
   ½ teaspoon salt (optional)
   ¼ teaspoon black pepper
   1 lemon, cut into 8 wedges

1. Remove any tough stems from kale. Stack several leaves; roll up. Cut crosswise into 1-inch slices. Repeat with remaining leaves.

2. Heat oil in large saucepan or Dutch oven over medium heat. Add garlic; cook 3 minutes, stirring occasionally. Add chopped kale and broth. Cover and simmer 7 minutes. Stir; reduce heat to medium-low. Cover and simmer 8 to 10 minutes or until kale is tender.

3. Stir in salt, if desired, and pepper. Serve with lemon wedges.   *Makes 8 servings*

nutrients per serving:

Calories 50
Calories from Fat 33%
Protein 2g
Carbohydrate 8g
Fiber 2g
Total Fat 2g
Saturated Fat <1g
Cholesterol 0mg
Sodium 32mg

Dietary Exchanges:
Vegetable 2
Fat ½

Grapefruit

Grapefruit's juicy, tart flavor and filling fiber make it a wonderful food to include in your meal plan. It is low in calories, too!

benefits

Grapefruit's soluble fiber helps stabilize blood sugar and lower cholesterol, which is often elevated in people with diabetes. It's rich in vitamin A, a vitamin essential for fending off infections and preventing vision problems, two categories of disease that are more common when blood sugar levels are consistently high. Grapefruit is also a good source of vitamin C and beta-carotene, both antioxidants, which research has shown can help prevent sight-stealing cataracts and macular degeneration. Because grapefruit and its juice may interfere with the actions of certain medications, be sure to read labels carefully and consult your physician and pharmacist.

selection and storage

Grapefruit isn't picked unless it's fully ripe, so no need to worry about ripeness. You'll want to choose grapefruit that feel heavy and avoid those that are soft, mushy or oblong rather than round. The difference in taste among white, red and pink varieties is minimal; they are equally sweet (and tart). Store grapefruit in your refrigerator's crisper drawer; they'll keep for up to two weeks.

preparation and serving tips

Wash grapefruit before cutting to prevent bacteria that might be on the skin from being introduced to the inside. You might want to bring grapefruit to room temperature before you juice or slice it for better flavor.

nutrients per serving:

Grapefruit
½ medium

Calories 41
Protein 1g
Total Fat 0g
Saturated Fat 0g
Cholesterol 0mg
Carbohydrate 10g
Dietary Fiber 1.5g
Sodium 0mg
Potassium 180mg
Calcium 15mg
Iron 0.1mg
Vitamin A 1,187 IU
Vitamin C 44mg
Folate 13mcg

Beyond the typical halved grapefruit at breakfast, try peeling and eating it out of hand for a juicy, mouthwatering snack.

citrus fruit toss

¼ cup dried cranberries

¼ cup water

2 cups red grapefruit sections, drained

2 tablespoons sucralose-based sugar substitute

2 tablespoons fresh mint leaves, chopped

1 tablespoon lime juice

1. Combine cranberries and water in medi... microwavable bowl. Microwave on HIGH 1 minute; let stand 5 minutes. Drain well.

2. Add grapefruit, sugar substitute, mint and lime juice; toss gently. Let stand 5 minutes before serving. *Makes 4 servings*

nutrients per serving:

Calories 74
Calories from Fat 2%
Protein <1g
Carbohydrate 20g
Fiber 2g
Total Fat <1g
Saturated Fat <1g
Cholesterol 0mg
Sodium <1mg

Dietary Exchanges:
Fruit 1

Greek Yogurt

This Mediterranean-style yogurt is creamier and thicker than regular yogurt and contains almost double the protein with fewer carbohydrates, making it a winner for people with diabetes.

benefits

If you're looking for a healthy, calcium-rich dairy food but need to watch your carbohydrate intake, Greek yogurt is a great choice. While regular yogurts have 15 to 17 grams of carbohydrates per 4-ounce serving, Greek yogurt averages around 9 grams, and some brands have even less. Because it is rich in lean protein, Greek yogurt provides long-lasting energy without a surge in blood sugar levels. A triple-straining process that removes more whey (liquid) is what makes Greek yogurt so creamy; it also lowers the lactose content, making this yogurt easier for some people to digest. Greek yogurt contains about 50 percent less sodium than regular yogurt, making it a better choice if you're also battling high blood pressure. Like regular varieties, Greek yogurt provides healthy bacteria, or probiotics, to help keep your immune system and digestive health in top form.

selection and storage

Greek yogurt is a newcomer to the yogurt aisle, but its growing popularity is bringing it to most supermarkets. Like regular yogurt, it is available in nonfat, low-fat and whole milk varieties; flavors include plain, vanilla, fruit varieties and Mediterranean-influenced honey. Like all yogurt, Greek yogurt should be stored in the refrigerator and used within about two weeks.

preparation and serving tips

Greek yogurt can be enjoyed straight from the carton or used as a base to make salad dressings, dips, sauces, smoothies, ice creams and desserts.

nutrients per serving:

Greek Yogurt, nonfat ½ cup

Calories 80
Protein 11g
Total Fat 0g
Saturated Fat 0g
Cholesterol 0mg
Carbohydrate 9g
Dietary Fiber 0g
Sodium 45mg
Potassium 160mg
Calcium 150mg

greek chickpea salad

- 4 cups packed baby spinach leaves
- 1 cup canned chickpeas, rinsed and drained
- 1 large shallot, thinly sliced
- 4 pitted kalamata olives, sliced
- 2 tablespoons crumbled reduced-fat feta cheese

Dressing

- ¼ cup plain nonfat Greek yogurt
- 2 teaspoons white wine vinegar
- 1 teaspoon olive oil
- 1 clove garlic, minced
- ¼ teaspoon black pepper
- ⅛ teaspoon salt

1. Combine spinach, chickpeas, shallot, olives and feta cheese in large bowl; toss gently.

2. Whisk yogurt, vinegar, oil, garlic, pepper and salt in small bowl. Spoon over salad just before serving; toss gently.

Makes 4 servings

Green Beans

Green beans, also known as snap beans, are a great vegetable choice for people with diabetes. Not only are they low in carbohydrates, their crunchy texture makes them a pleasure to eat—a double bonus.

nutrients per serving:

Green Beans
½ cup cooked

Calories 22
Protein 1g
Total Fat 0g
Saturated Fat 0g
Cholesterol 0mg
Carbohydrate 5g
Dietary Fiber 2g
Sodium 0mg
Potassium 90mg
Calcium 28mg
Chromium 1mcg
Iron 0.4mg
Vitamin A 438 IU
Vitamin C 6mg
Folate 21mcg

benefits

Green beans are low in calories and carbohydrates, so they're less likely to have a negative effect on your blood sugar or waistline.

Additionally, they provide essential vitamins, minerals and fiber. Green beans contain chromium, a mineral that is known to enhance the action of insulin. Green beans are also rich in some carotenoids, such as beta-carotene and lutein. Lutein appears to help protect the eyes from damage and disease, including the vision complications associated with diabetes.

selection and storage

Fresh green beans are at their peak from May to October. Choose slender beans that are crisp, brightly colored and without blemishes. Store them in a plastic bag in the refrigerator for up to five days. Frozen green beans are available and come very close nutritionally. Canned green beans are also an option but may lose some vitamins during processing and typically contain more sodium.

preparation and serving tips

Fresh or frozen green beans can be steamed lightly on the stove or in the microwave just until crisp-tender. Canned green beans can be rinsed to lower the sodium and should be heated gently to prevent them from getting mushy. Green beans stand up well on their own as a side dish, lightly seasoned with herbs or sprinkled with toasted nuts. Or add green beans to soups or casseroles. Raw green beans make a great snack with a low-fat dip.

balsamic green beans with almonds

- 1 pound fresh green beans, trimmed
- 2 teaspoons olive oil
- 2 teaspoons balsamic vinegar
- ½ teaspoon salt
- ¼ teaspoon black pepper
- 2 tablespoons sliced almonds, toasted*

Toast almonds in small skillet over medium heat 3 to 5 minutes or until fragrant, stirring frequently.

1. Place beans in medium saucepan; add enough water to cover. Bring to a simmer over high heat. Reduce heat; simmer, uncovered, 4 to 8 minutes or until beans are crisp-tender. (Cooking time will vary depending on thickness of beans.) Drain well and return to saucepan.

2. Add oil, vinegar, salt and pepper; toss to coat. Sprinkle with almonds just before serving. *Makes 4 servings*

nutrients per serving:

Calories 87
Calories from Fat 51%
Protein 3g
Carbohydrate 9g
Fiber 4g
Total Fat 5g
Saturated Fat <1g
Cholesterol 0mg
Sodium 297mg

Dietary Exchanges:
Vegetable 1½
Fat 1

Green Peas

Peas, also known as English or garden peas, are considered a starchy vegetable, but their high fiber and protein contents make them ideal for people with diabetes.

benefits

Among fresh vegetables, green peas are one of the richest in fiber, most of it soluble. Soluble fiber helps slow absorption of glucose (sugar) from food, preventing wild blood sugar spikes and keeping the blood sugar levels steady. Green peas are a low-calorie, low-fat source of protein, offering twice the amount of protein of most other vegetables. They can therefore be a beneficial addition to vegetarian entrées, as they supply long-lasting energy. Green peas also contain antioxidants vitamin C and lutein, a plant pigment that helps prevent eye diseases associated with diabetes.

selection and storage

Fresh green peas are available in the spring and fall. Choose those that are firm, plump and bright green. Because their sugar quickly turns to starch, the sooner you eat them the more flavorful they'll be. Store fresh peas in the refrigerator, but eat them within a few days. Green peas are available frozen and canned, which are just as nutritious as fresh. Be sure to rinse canned peas to lower the sodium content.

preparation and serving tips

Wash fresh peas just before shelling. Steam fresh or frozen green peas for a very short time, 6 to 8 minutes, to retain flavor and vitamin C content. Canned peas only need gentle heating to prevent them from getting mushy. Peas are versatile enough to be added to many dishes, raw or cooked. Use them in salads, soups and casseroles, or simply enjoy as a side dish alone or mixed with other vegetables.

Don't be a stranger to this root vegetable. Often referred to as a Mexican potato, jicama is refreshingly crisp and crunchy, with a sweet, nutty flavor and radishlike texture.

Jicama

benefits

Foods like jicama that have a high water content and ample fiber help prevent sudden, large shifts in blood sugar levels. Such foods also fill you up without piling on calories and fats, helping with any weight-loss efforts. Plus, jicama provides vitamin C, which research suggests can help protect arteries from damage that can lead to heart attacks and strokes.

selection and storage

Jicama is available in many large supermarkets from November through May.

Select jicama that is firm and unblemished with a slightly silky sheen. It should not feel soft or appear to have bruises or wrinkles, which signal that it has been stored for too long. Jicama can be stored for up to two weeks in a plastic bag in the refrigerator.

preparation and serving tips

Jicama is a versatile vegetable that adds a crisp texture and nutty sweetness to foods; it also tends to take on flavors of the foods that it accompanies. The thin skin of jicama should be peeled before eating or cooking. Cut jicama into cubes or sticks and add it to salads, salsa or coleslaw. It can also be added to stir-fries or roasted with other vegetables. You may simply enjoy it alone as a

snack with a low-fat dip. For a refreshing salad, combine cubed jicama, sliced cucumber and orange sections and sprinkle with chili powder, salt and a drizzle of fresh lemon juice.

nutrients per serving:

Jicama
½ cup raw

Calories 25
Protein <1g
Total Fat 0g
Saturated Fat 0g
Cholesterol 0mg
Carbohydrate 6g
Dietary Fiber 3g
Sodium 5mg
Potassium 100mg
Calcium 8mg
Iron 0.4mg
Vitamin A 14 IU
Vitamin C 13mg
Folate 8mcg

Leeks

These large green onion look-alikes are related to both onions and garlic and have a mellow, slightly sweet flavor. They're great for adding a touch of satisfying flavor in place of fat- and calorie-laden sauces, butter or excess salt.

benefits

Leeks are a caloric bargain: One serving provides an appreciable amount of nutrients for less than 20 calories. What makes them even better for people with diabetes is that they are a nonstarchy vegetable, meaning they're low in sugars and carbohydrates that make blood sugar levels jump. Like onions and garlic, leeks contain heart-protecting phytonutrients, which may have a mild blood pressure-lowering effect as well as help prevent blood clots that can block arteries and cause heart attacks and strokes, common killers of people with diabetes.

selection and storage

Leeks are available year-round. Choose those with crisp, bright green leaves and an unblemished white portion. Smaller leeks will be more tender. Refrigerate leeks in a plastic bag for up to five days.

preparation and serving tips

Slit leeks from top to bottom and wash thoroughly to remove dirt trapped between leaf layers. Although the entire leek is edible, most people prefer to eat the white fleshy base and tender inner leaves and discard the bitter dark green leaves. Try using leeks in place of onions for added flavor in soups or vegetable dishes. You can also add them to salads and salad dressings. They make a tasty and healthy side dish when sautéed or grilled in a little olive oil or light butter.

nutrients per serving:

Leeks
½ cup cooked

Calories 16
Protein <1g

Total Fat 0g
Saturated Fat 0g
Cholesterol 0mg
Carbohydrate 4g
Dietary Fiber 0.5g
Sodium 5mg
Potassium 45mg

Calcium 16mg
Iron 0.6mg
Vitamin A 422 IU
Vitamin C 2mg
Folate 12mcg

spring vegetable ragoût

1 tablespoon olive oil
2 leeks, thinly sliced
3 cloves garlic, minced
1 package (10 ounces) frozen corn
8 ounces yellow squash, halved
    lengthwise and cut into
    ½-inch pieces (about 1¼ cups)
1 cup vegetable broth
1 small bag (6 ounces) frozen
    edamame, shelled
1 small bag (4 ounces) shredded
    carrots
3 cups small cherry tomatoes,
    halved
1 teaspoon dried tarragon
1 teaspoon dried basil
1 teaspoon dried oregano
    Salt and black pepper (optional)
    Minced fresh parsley (optional)

1. Heat oil in large skillet over medium heat. Add leeks and garlic; cook and stir just until fragrant. Add corn, squash, broth, edamame and carrots; cook and stir until squash is tender.

2. Add tomatoes, tarragon, basil and oregano; stir well. Reduce heat; cover and simmer 2 minutes or until tomatoes are soft. Season with salt and pepper, if desired. Garnish with parsley.

Makes 6 servings

Lemons

Lemons' tart juice and zesty peel add life to everything from fish and vegetables to tea and water, helping to perk up the fresh, healthy foods in your diabetic meal plan.

benefits

Lemons are loaded with vitamin C, which is essential for controlling infections; that is especially important to people with diabetes, who are at increased risk for a variety of infections. As an antioxidant, vitamin C also helps to fight inflammation, which is suspected of playing a role not only in the development of diabetes but also in its progression and complications. Lemons' zest, or outer peel, is rich in another antioxidant, rutin, which may help strengthen blood vessel walls and protect them from damage.

selection and storage

Lemon varieties vary mostly in their skin thickness, juiciness and number of seeds. Look for firm, unblemished lemons that are heavy for their size—an indicator of juiciness. Thin-skinned fruits yield the most juice. Refrigerated, they keep for a month or two.

preparation and serving tips

To get more juice from a lemon, bring it to room temperature, then roll it back and forth under the palm of your hand before you cut and squeeze it. Another flavorful part of the fruit is its zest. Scrape it off with a grater, knife or zester and use it to enhance desserts and fruit salads. Be sure to wash lemons thoroughly before grating the peel or cutting into the fruit. Lemon adds a flavorful zing to fish and bean dishes, helping to reduce the need for unhealthy sauces and seasonings.

nutrients per serving:

Lemon juice of 1 medium

Calories 12
Protein <1g
Total Fat 0g
Saturated Fat 0g
Cholesterol 0mg
Carbohydrate 4g
Dietary Fiber 0.2g
Sodium 0mg
Potassium 58mg
Calcium 3mg
Vitamin A 9 IU
Vitamin C 22mg
Folate 6mcg

asparagus with lemon & mustard

    12 fresh asparagus spears
    2 tablespoons fat-free mayonnaise
    1 tablespoon brown mustard
    1 tablespoon lemon juice
    1 teaspoon grated lemon peel, divided

1. Fill large saucepan with 1 inch water; bring to a boil over high heat. Place asparagus in steamer basket; steam until crisp-tender. Rinse under cold water; drain and chill.

2. Combine mayonnaise, mustard and lemon juice in small bowl. Stir in 1/2 teaspoon lemon peel.

3. Divide asparagus between two plates. Spoon 2 tablespoons dressing over each serving. Top with remaining 1/2 teaspoon lemon peel.

Makes 2 servings

nutrients per serving:

Calories 39
Calories from Fat 14%
Protein 3g
Carbohydrate 7g
Fiber 2g
Total Fat 1g
Saturated Fat <1g
Cholesterol 0mg
Sodium 294mg

Dietary Exchanges:
Vegetable 1½

Lentils

Because they are loaded with nutrients, lentils are finally gaining the recognition they deserve as a great source of low-fat protein and a wonderful meat substitute.

benefits

Because people with diabetes have to control their carbohydrate intake, they need to choose carbohydrate foods that deliver the most nutritional bang without sending their blood sugar levels skyrocketing. Legumes fit the bill perfectly as they are a great source of several essential vitamins and minerals, protein and fiber. Their soluble fiber slows their digestion, preventing a big spike in blood sugar; it also lowers blood cholesterol, which can help decrease the higher risk of heart disease associated with diabetes.

selection and storage

Brown, green and red lentils are the most common varieties in the United States. If you buy them packaged, look for well-sealed bags with uniformly sized, brightly colored, disc-shaped lentils. If you buy them in bulk, beware of holes, which indicate insect infestation. Lentils keep for up to a year when stored in a well-sealed container at a cool temperature.

preparation and serving tips

Red lentils cook quickly and become mushy, so they work best in soups, purées or dips. Brown and green lentils retain their shape when cooked and can be used in salads or any dish in which you don't want your lentils to be very soft. Most lentils will cook in 30 to 45 minutes and don't require a precooking soak like dried beans do. Best of all, lentils are willing recipients of flavorful herbs and spices, taking on the flavors of the foods they are mixed with.

nutrients per serving:

Lentils
½ cup cooked

Calories 115
Protein 9g
Total Fat 0g
Saturated Fat 0g
Cholesterol 0mg
Carbohydrate 20g
Dietary Fiber 8g
Sodium 0mg
Potassium 365mg
Calcium 19mg
Iron 3.3mg
Vitamin A 8 IU
Vitamin C 2mg
Folate 179mcg

lentil chili

- 1 tablespoon canola oil
- 4 cloves garlic, minced
- 1 tablespoon chili powder
- 1 package (32 ounces) reduced-sodium vegetable broth
- ¾ cup dried brown or green lentils, rinsed and sorted
- 2 teaspoons smoked chipotle hot pepper sauce
- 2 cups peeled and diced butternut squash
- 1 can (about 14 ounces) no-salt added diced tomatoes
- ½ cup chopped fresh cilantro
- ¼ cup pepitas (pumpkin seeds) (optional)

1. Heat oil in large saucepan over medium heat. Add garlic; cook and stir 1 minute. Add chili powder; cook and stir 30 seconds.

2. Add broth, lentils and hot pepper sauce; bring to a boil over high heat. Reduce heat to low; simmer 15 minutes. Stir in squash and tomatoes; simmer 18 to 20 minutes or until lentils and squash are tender.

3. Top with cilantro and pepitas, if desired, just before serving. *Makes 5 servings*

nutrients per serving:

Calories 184
Calories from Fat 15%
Protein 10g
Carbohydrate 32g
Fiber 12g
Total Fat 3g
Saturated Fat <1g

Cholesterol 0mg
Sodium 322mg

Dietary Exchanges:
Starch 2
Meat 1

Lettuce

Lettuce is the ultimate when it comes to getting a nutritional bang for your calorie buck. Lettuce offers a variety of essential nutrients for very few calories.

nutrients per serving:

Lettuce, romaine 1 cup

Calories 8
Protein 1g
Total Fat 0g
Saturated Fat 0g
Cholesterol 0mg
Carbohydrate 2g
Dietary Fiber 1g
Sodium 5mg
Potassium 115mg
Calcium 16mg
Iron 0.5mg
Vitamin A 4,094 IU
Vitamin C 11mg
Folate 64mcg

benefits

The key to making lettuce a valuable part of your diabetic meal plan is to choose varieties with dark green or other deeply colored leaves. This way, you get valuable nutrients, such as vitamin C, which helps your body fight off infection. Lettuce also contains vitamin A and the antioxidants lutein and zeaxanthin, which help protect your vision from sight-stealing diabetes complications. And the folate in lettuce helps to protect your heart.

selection and storage

There are hundreds of varieties of lettuce available in the supermarket. Nutrient-rich varieties include romaine, endive, escarole, looseleaf, butterhead, arugula and watercress. Choose lettuce that is crisp and free of blemishes. Lettuce should be stored in the refrigerator for up to five days. Prewashed salad greens are a convenient option.

preparation and serving tips

For heads of lettuce, remove the leaves, wash and either drain completely or blot with a paper towel to remove excess moisture. Lettuce can be combined with fresh fruits or vegetables, cold pasta or chunks of chicken or tuna to make low-calorie, highly nutritious main dishes. Just go easy on the salad dressing and high-calorie toppings. For a side dish, make a salad with a variety of deep green lettuces with olive oil and a little flavored vinegar or lemon juice.

asian lettuce wraps with hoisin dipping sauce

Sauce

- ¼ cup hoisin sauce
- ¼ cup pomegranate juice
- 1 teaspoon sugar
- 1 teaspoon grated orange peel

Wraps

- 4 cups coleslaw mix or broccoli slaw mix
- 1½ cups frozen shelled edamame, thawed
- 1 cup matchstick carrots
- 1 medium jalapeño pepper,* seeded and sliced into thin strips
- ¼ cup chopped fresh cilantro
- 1½ cups diced cooked chicken
- 2 ounces toasted peanuts
- 12 leaves Bibb or romaine lettuce

*Jalapeño peppers can sting and irritate the skin, so wear rubber gloves when handling peppers and do not touch your eyes.

1. Combine sauce ingredients in small bowl; set aside.

2. Combine coleslaw mix, edamame, carrots, jalapeño and cilantro in medium bowl. Reserve 3 cups slaw mixture and ¼ cup sauce; cover and refrigerate for another use.

3. Add chicken and peanuts to remaining slaw mixture and toss gently. Arrange lettuce leaves on large platter. Spoon about ⅓ cup mixture on top of each lettuce leaf and drizzle 1 teaspoon sauce over each.   *Makes 4 servings*

nutrients per serving:

Calories 198
Calories from Fat 36%
Protein 14g
Carbohydrate 20g
Fiber 4g

Total Fat 8g
Saturated Fat 1g
Cholesterol 25mg
Sodium 176mg

Dietary Exchanges:
Starch 1
Meat 1
Fat 1

Lima Beans

Because they have such a delicate, buttery flavor, lima beans are also known as butter beans. What makes them more enjoyable is that they are one of the lowest in calories and highest in fiber of all of the various types of beans.

benefits

Lima beans' high fiber content helps keep blood sugar levels from spiking after a meal and can help lower blood cholesterol levels, making these legumes an excellent dietary choice for people with diabetes. They also provide potassium and magnesium, which may help combat high blood pressure. Combine lima beans with a whole grain such as rice, and you get a meal that is full of high-quality protein and is virtually fat free.

selection and storage

Lima beans are pale green, plump-bodied and have a rounded kidney shape. There are two varieties, baby lima and Fordhook. The Fordhook is larger,

plumper and has a fuller flavor. Both varieties can be found sold in their pods during the summer months. Store them in the refrigerator and shell just before using. Frozen, canned and dried lima beans can be used in place of fresh and are available year-round.

preparation and serving tips

To prepare lima beans, cook in a saucepan or in the microwave with a small amount of water until tender. They work great in soups and make an excellent side dish with some olive oil and garlic. Lima beans are in the traditional Native American dish succotash, which combines this delicious bean with corn. Try it with a twist: Fill corn tortillas with lima beans and corn kernels and top with chopped tomatoes, avocado and scallions.

nutrients per serving:

Lima Beans
½ cup cooked

Calories 105
Protein 6g
Total Fat 0g

Saturated Fat 0g
Cholesterol 0mg
Carbohydrate 20g
Dietary Fiber 4.5g
Sodium 15mg
Potassium 485mg

Calcium 27mg
Iron 2.1mg
Magnesium 63mg
Phosphorus 110mg
Folate 22mcg

skillet succotash

 1 teaspoon canola oil
½ cup diced onion
½ cup diced green bell pepper
½ cup diced celery
½ teaspoon paprika
¾ cup frozen corn
¾ cup frozen lima beans
½ cup canned low-sodium diced tomatoes
 1 teaspoon dried parsley flakes *or*
   1 tablespoon minced fresh parsley
¼ teaspoon salt
¼ teaspoon black pepper

1. Heat oil in large skillet over medium heat.
Add onion, bell pepper and celery; cook and stir
5 minutes or until onion is translucent and bell
pepper and celery are crisp-tender. Stir in paprika.

2. Add corn, lima beans and tomatoes; reduce heat.
Cover and simmer 20 minutes or until beans are
tender. Stir in parsley, salt and black pepper.

Makes 4 servings

Tip: For additional flavor, add 1 clove minced garlic
and 1 bay leaf to the onion mixture. Remove and
discard bay leaf before serving.

nutrients per serving:

Calories 99
Calories from Fat 14%
Protein 4g
Carbohydrate 19g
Fiber 4g
Total Fat 2g
Saturated Fat <1g
Cholesterol 0mg
Sodium 187mg

Dietary Exchanges:
Starch 1
Fat ½

Limes

Using lime juice in cooking is an easy, healthy way to perk up any dish. Just add a splash with a few herbs, and your meal will be full of flavor but not calories.

benefits

Lime juice provides a ton of flavor for very few calories and carbohydrates. Limes also contain a hefty amount of vitamin C, helping the body fight infections. This is important for people with diabetes, as infections tend to develop more easily due to damage to the nerves and blood vessels by high blood sugar levels. Additionally, the powerful phytochemicals found in limes may help protect cells from damage that can lead to heart disease.

selection and storage

The Persian lime is the most common variety found. The key lime—the star in the famous tropical dessert—is small and round, while the Persian looks more like a green lemon. Key limes are generally more flavorful due to their greater acidity. Limes typically turn yellowish as they ripen. The greenest limes have the best flavor. Refrigerated, they keep for about a month.

preparation and serving tips

Lime juice can be used as a salt substitute for meat and fish dishes, and a splash of lime juice over fruit prevents discoloration while adding a zing of flavor. To get more juice from a lime, bring it to room temperature, then roll it back and forth under the palm of your hand before you cut and squeeze it. Lime peel is often used to add flavor to salads, sauces and desserts.

nutrients per serving:

Lime
juice of 1 medium

Calories 11
Protein 0g
Total Fat 0g
Saturated Fat 0g
Cholesterol 0mg
Carbohydrate 4g
Dietary Fiber 0g
Sodium 1mg
Potassium 51.5mg
Calcium 6.2mg
Vitamin A 22 IU
Vitamin C 13.2mg
Folate 4.4mcg

grilled chicken adobo

½ cup chopped onion
⅓ cup lime juice
6 cloves garlic, coarsely chopped
1 teaspoon ground cumin
1 teaspoon dried oregano
½ teaspoon dried thyme
¼ teaspoon ground red pepper
6 boneless skinless chicken breasts
    (about ¼ pound each)
3 tablespoons chopped fresh cilantro (optional)

1. Combine onion, lime juice and garlic in food processor; process until onion is finely minced. Transfer to resealable food storage bag. Add cumin, oregano, thyme and red pepper; knead bag until blended. Place chicken in bag; press out air and seal. Turn to coat chicken with marinade. Refrigerate 30 minutes or up to 4 hours, turning occasionally.

2. Spray grid with nonstick cooking spray. Prepare grill for direct cooking. Remove chicken from marinade; discard marinade. Grill chicken over medium heat 5 to 7 minutes on each side or until no longer pink in center. Garnish with cilantro.

Makes 6 servings

nutrients per serving:

Calories 139
Calories from Fat 19%
Protein 25g
Carbohydrate 1g
Fiber <1g
Total Fat 3g
Saturated Fat <1g
Cholesterol 69mg
Sodium 61mg

Dietary Exchanges:
Meat 3

Milk

Known best for its role in bone health and for its high calcium and protein contents, milk's rich nutrients make it great for a diabetic diet.

benefits

Vitamin D has recently been found to not only play a role in bone health but also play a part in regulating blood sugar levels. A growing body of evidence indicates that a deficiency in vitamin D can increase the risk of type 2 diabetes as well as diabetes-related complications. Furthermore, people with diabetes who don't get enough vitamin D have close to double the risk of heart disease and a greater risk of heart attack and stroke than people with diabetes with adequate levels. Fortunately, it is easy to get vitamin D from fortified milk.

selection and storage

Milk varies in the percentage of fat, from whole (4%) to reduced-fat (2%), low-fat (1%) and fat-free (skim). There are significant fat and calorie savings between whole and fat-free milk, but no difference in other nutrients. To capture the most benefits, choose milk fortified with vitamins A and D. All milk containers have a "sell-by" date, and the milk will stay fresh about seven days after this date. Avoid raw, or unpasteurized, milk, as it may carry harmful bacteria.

preparation and serving tips

Milk tastes best when served icy cold. It is rich in protein, making it filling and satisfying no matter how you enjoy it. Drink it alone as a snack or with a meal. Enjoy it with cereal or in a smoothie with your favorite fruits for a sweet, satisfying meal. Most recipes that call for milk, like soups and casseroles, work fine with low-fat milk varieties.

nutrients per serving:

Milk, fat-free (skim)
1 cup

Calories 83		Sodium 105mg
Protein 8g		Potassium 380mg
Total Fat 0g		Calcium 299mg
Saturated Fat 0g		Vitamin A 500 IU
Cholesterol 5mg		Vitamin D 115 IU
Carbohydrate 12g		Folate 12mcg
Dietary Fiber 0g		

peachy vanilla smoothie

¾ cup fat-free (skim) milk
½ cup crushed ice
¼ cup plain nonfat yogurt
1 medium peach, peeled and pitted
1 tablespoon sugar substitute
¼ teaspoon vanilla

Combine milk, ice, yogurt, peach, sugar substitute and vanilla in blender; blend until smooth. Serve immediately.

Makes 1 serving

nutrients per serving:

Calories 160
Calories from Fat 0%
Protein 11g
Carbohydrate 29g
Fiber 2g
Total Fat 0g
Saturated Fat 0g
Cholesterol 5mg
Sodium 120mg

Dietary Exchanges:
Fruit 1
Milk 1

Mushrooms

Mushrooms can be enjoyed in countless ways, but their hearty texture makes them best served as a low-calorie meat substitute.

nutrients per serving:

Mushrooms
½ cup cooked

Calories 22
Protein 2g
Total Fat 1g
Saturated Fat 0g
Cholesterol 0mg
Carbohydrate 4g
Dietary Fiber 2g
Sodium 0mg
Potassium 278mg
Calcium 5mg
Iron 1.4mg
Vitamin D 16.4 IU
Selenium 9mcg
Niacin 3.5mg
Riboflavin 0.2mg

benefits

Mushrooms are essentially a "free food" in a diabetic diet, as they are very low in calories and carbohydrates. They are also virtually sodium free and provide a hefty amount of potassium, which benefits the many people with diabetes who also have high blood pressure. What makes mushrooms stand out is that they are the only source of vitamin D found in the produce aisle. Many varieties of mushrooms are also rich in selenium, a mineral with anticancer properties.

selection and storage

All supermarkets stock the white button mushroom, and many have expanded their selection to include other varieties, such as shiitake, chanterelle, enoki, morel, oyster, portobello and the often dried Chinese wood-ear. Mushrooms like cool, humid, circulating air and need to be stored in a paper bag or ventilated container in your refrigerator, but not in the crisper drawer. Mushrooms last only a couple of days but can still be used to impart flavor in cooking after they've turned brown.

preparation and serving tips

To clean, use a mushroom brush or wipe mushrooms with a damp cloth. Don't cut mushrooms until you're ready to use them. Mushrooms cook quickly. They'll absorb oil in cooking, so it's best to sauté mushrooms in broth or wine. Try going meatless sometimes; portobello mushrooms are good for grilling and can take the place of meat in many dishes, including burgers and meat loaves.

stuffed portobellos with sausage

- 4 portobello mushroom caps
  Nonstick cooking spray
- 6 ounces reduced-fat bulk sausage
- 1 cup chopped yellow onion
- 1 medium red bell pepper, chopped
- 1 medium zucchini, chopped
- 1 teaspoon dried thyme
- 2 slices whole wheat bread, grated in blender or hand grater (about 1 cup)
- ½ cup chopped fresh parsley
- ⅓ cup water
  Salt (optional)

1. Preheat oven to 350°F. Remove stem from each mushroom cap. Chop stems; set aside.

2. Spray both sides of each mushroom cap with cooking spray. Place on baking sheet; set aside.

3. Spray large nonstick skillet with cooking spray; heat over medium-high heat. Add sausage; cook until browned, stirring to break up large pieces. Drain sausage on paper towels.

4. Add onion, bell pepper, zucchini, mushroom stems and thyme to skillet; cook and stir 4 minutes or until onion is translucent. Remove skillet from heat. Stir in sausage, bread crumbs, parsley, water and salt, if desired.

5. Top each mushroom cap with ¾ cup filling; cover with foil. Bake 30 minutes or until tender. Let stand 5 minutes before serving to allow flavors to blend. *Makes 4 servings*

nutrients per serving:

Calories 139
Calories from Fat 19%
Protein 9g
Carbohydrate 20g
Fiber 4g
Total Fat 3g
Saturated Fat 1g
Cholesterol 19mg
Sodium 465mg

Dietary Exchanges:
Vegetable 2
Starch ½
Meat 1

Mustard Greens

Mustard greens and their cousins—beet, collard, dandelion and turnip greens—are gaining recognition as nutrition powerhouses, having more antioxidants than many common fruits and vegetables. Peppery mustard greens are one of the most nutritious of all the leafy greens.

benefits

All leafy greens are loaded with powerful phytonutrients, and research shows an extra daily serving could help decrease the risk of type 2 diabetes and diabetes complications. Mustard greens are full of folate, beta-carotene and vitamin C, all of which support the health of the heart and blood vessels. They also contain soluble fiber, which helps lower blood cholesterol levels and fight hunger.

selection and storage

Look for fresh mustard greens with crisp, dark green leaves. Choose small leaves and avoid those that are sunken, spotted or discolored. Store unwashed greens in the refrigerator. They will last three to five days but should be eaten soon after purchase as they develop a strong bitter flavor over time. Mustard greens are also available frozen or canned and can be used in place of fresh in many dishes.

preparation and serving tips

Wash greens well and remove the tough stems. Mustard greens can be steamed, sautéed or simmered until wilted. For a tasty side dish, simmer in broth and season with onion and garlic. Combine mustard greens with other vegetables in stir-fries. Frozen or canned mustard greens work great in soups and stews.

nutrients per serving:

Mustard Greens
½ cup cooked

Calories 10
Protein 2g

Total Fat 0g
Saturated Fat 0g
Cholesterol 0mg
Carbohydrate 2g
Dietary Fiber 1.5g
Sodium 10mg
Potassium 140mg

Calcium 52mg
Iron 0.5mg
Vitamin A 4,426 IU
Vitamin C 18mg
Folate 51mcg

garlicky mustard greens

- 2 pounds mustard greens
- 1 teaspoon olive oil
- 1 cup chopped onion
- 2 cloves garlic, minced
- ¾ cup chopped red bell pepper
- ½ cup fat-free reduced-sodium chicken or vegetable broth
- 1 tablespoon cider vinegar
- 1 teaspoon sugar

1. Remove stems and any wilted leaves from greens. Stack several leaves; roll up. Cut crosswise into 1-inch slices. Repeat with remaining leaves.

2. Heat oil in large saucepan over medium heat. Add onion and garlic; cook and stir 5 minutes or until onion is translucent. Stir in greens, bell pepper and broth. Reduce heat to low. Cover and cook 25 minutes or until greens are tender, stirring occasionally.

3. Whisk vinegar and sugar in small bowl until sugar is dissolved. Stir into cooked greens. Serve immediately. *Makes 4 servings*

nutrients per serving:

Calories 72
Calories from Fat 25%
Protein 6g
Carbohydrate 11g
Fiber 5g

Total Fat 2g
Saturated Fat <1g
Cholesterol 0mg
Sodium 42mg

Dietary Exchanges:
Vegetable 2½

Nectarines

For a healthy way to satisfy your sweet tooth, try a juicy nectarine. Named for its delicious nectar, this fruit is a wonderful low-calorie treat.

benefits

The flesh of the nectarine is a rich source of soluble fiber, the kind that slows the absorption of sugar, preventing blood sugar levels from fluctuating. Nectarines' generous fiber content can also help lower blood cholesterol levels.

Additionally, nectarines can help prevent diabetes-related complications; they contain beta-carotene, an antioxidant that converts to vitamin A in the body, which plays an essential role in eye health.

selection and storage

Nectarines look like peaches without the fuzz, but you'll also find a variation known as a white nectarine with lighter skin and flesh. Nectarines are at their best from midspring to early fall. Choose nectarines that are firm yet give slightly to the touch. Avoid those with bruises or blemishes as well as those that are hard or overly green. Slightly underripe nectarines will ripen at room temperature within a couple of days. Refrigerate to help slow ripening, but use within five days.

preparations and serving tips

A ripe nectarine is a juicy treat, whether eaten out of hand or sliced from the pit. Nectarines make a delicious addition to salads and can be used in a variety of fresh or cooked desserts. The flesh will darken when exposed to air, so be sure to sprinkle with lemon juice to prevent browning when served in fresh salads or desserts.

nutrients per serving:

**Nectarine
1 medium**

Calories 62
Protein 2g
Total Fat 0g
Saturated Fat 0g
Cholesterol 0mg
Carbohydrate 15g
Dietary Fiber 2.5g
Sodium 0mg
Potassium 285mg
Calcium 9mg
Vitamin A 471 IU
Vitamin C 8mg
Folate 7mcg

asian-inspired pork & nectarine kabobs

1 pound pork tenderloin
¾ cup pineapple juice
3 tablespoons reduced-sodium soy sauce
1 tablespoon grated fresh ginger
1 teaspoon minced garlic
1 teaspoon ground cumin
1 teaspoon chili powder
½ teaspoon black pepper
3 medium nectarines

1. Cut pork tenderloin lengthwise in half. Cut each half into eight pieces. Place pork in resealable food storage bag.

2. Whisk pineapple juice, soy sauce, ginger, garlic, cumin, chili powder and pepper in small bowl. Pour over pork; seal bag. Turn to coat pork completely. Marinate in refrigerator 3 to 6 hours.

3. Prepare grill for direct cooking.

4. Cut each nectarine into eight chunks. Drain pork, discarding marinade. Thread pork and nectarine pieces onto eight wooden skewers.* Grill over medium heat 9 to 12 minutes or until pork is barely pink in center, turning once.

Makes 4 servings

Soak wooden skewers in water 20 minutes before using to prevent burning.

nutrients per serving:

Calories 211
Calories from Fat 15%
Protein 25g
Carbohydrate 20g
Fiber 2g
Total Fat 4g
Saturated Fat 1g
Cholesterol 67mg
Sodium 429mg

Dietary Exchanges:
Fruit 1
Meat 3

Oats

All oats—instant, quick, old-fashioned and steel-cut—are beneficial for people with diabetes. They have a fiber-rich bran layer and are full of an array of nutrients.

benefits

Oats are best known for their soluble fiber, which slows the digestion of food and the absorption of nutrients to prevent blood sugar spikes. Choosing high-fiber foods like oats is essential for people with diabetes, as high blood sugar levels can damage many of the body's nerves and cells. In studies, a diet rich in soluble fiber improved the condition of people with diabetes so much that they were able to get off the medications they were taking for the disease.

selection and storage

Cooking time and texture are the only differences among the varieties of oats. Chewy steel-cut oats are whole oats sliced into thick pieces and take about 20 minutes to cook. Old-fashioned oats are steamed and flattened and take about 5 minutes to cook. Quick oats are cut into smaller pieces before being rolled and cook in about a minute. Instant oats are precooked, so it takes only boiling water to reconstitute them. Instant oats may have added sodium, and flavored versions have added sugar. Store in a dark, dry location in a well-sealed container for up to a year.

preparation and serving tips

Oats are commonly used as breakfast cereal or to make cookies, but they can also be used to boost fiber in many dishes, including meat loaves, burgers and fish patties. Grind oats in a blender or food processor and use to thicken soups or sauces or as a partial substitute for flour in baked goods.

nutrients per serving:

Oats
½ cup cooked

Calories 83
Protein 3g
Total Fat 2g
Saturated Fat 0g
Cholesterol 0mg
Carbohydrate 14g
Dietary Fiber 2g
Sodium 5mg
Potassium 80mg
Calcium 11mg
Iron 1.1mg
Magnesium 32mg
Manganese 0.7mg
Niacin 0.3mg

yummy breakfast cookies

- 1 cup all-purpose flour
- ¾ cup whole wheat flour
- 1 teaspoon baking powder
- 1 teaspoon baking soda
- 1 teaspoon ground cinnamon
- ½ teaspoon salt
- 1 cup (2 sticks) butter
- 1 cup crunchy peanut butter
- ¾ cup granulated sugar
- ¾ cup packed brown sugar
- 2 eggs
- 1 teaspoon vanilla
- 1¾ cups quick oats
- 1¼ cups raisins
- 1 medium Granny Smith apple, finely grated
- ⅓ cup finely grated carrot

1. Preheat oven to 350°F. Combine all-purpose flour, whole wheat flour, baking powder, baking soda, cinnamon and salt in medium bowl.

2. Beat butter, peanut butter, granulated sugar and brown sugar in large bowl with electric mixer at medium speed 2 minutes or until light and fluffy. Add eggs; beat 1 minute. Add flour mixture; beat at low speed until blended. Stir in oats, raisins, apple and carrot.

3. Drop by tablespoonfuls onto ungreased baking sheets. Bake 12 to 15 minutes or just until browned around edges. Cool on baking sheets 2 minutes. Remove to wire racks to cool completely.

Makes 48 servings

Tip: Freeze cookies between sheets of waxed paper in a sealed container. Thaw as needed for breakfast on the run or as a nutritious snack.

nutrients per serving:

Calories 109
Calories from Fat 46%
Protein 2g
Carbohydrate 13g
Fiber 1g
Total Fat 6g
Saturated Fat 1g

Cholesterol 7mg
Sodium 51mg

Dietary Exchanges:
Starch 1
Fat 1

Okra

Popular in southern cooking, okra offers a lot of benefits. This flavorful and filling vegetable has very few calories—just what the doctor ordered when you need to lose weight to improve blood sugar control.

nutrients per serving:

Okra
½ cup cooked

Calories 18
Protein 2g
Total Fat 0g
Saturated Fat 0g
Cholesterol 0mg
Carbohydrate 4g
Dietary Fiber 2g
Sodium 5mg
Potassium 110mg
Calcium 62mg
Iron 0.2mg
Vitamin A 226 IU
Vitamin C 13mg
Folate 37mcg

benefits

Okra is great for people with diabetes as it is packed with soluble fiber, which helps your body better regulate blood sugar levels by slowing the absorption of sugar from food. Okra's soluble fiber has a similar effect on cholesterol absorption, giving the body a leg up in its efforts to combat heart disease. Okra provides decent amounts of vitamins A and C and folate, which are also important in heart health.

selection and storage

Fresh okra has green-ridged skin and a tapered, oblong pod. It's usually available from about May through October but can also be found year-round canned and frozen. When buying fresh, look for smaller, firm, brightly colored pods; longer pods may be tough and fibrous. Avoid those that are dull in color, limp or blemished. Once at home, refrigerate them and use within five days.

preparation and serving tips

Rinse okra before cooking to remove dirt or residue; trim the crown end and tips. It can be sliced into small circular sections or cooked whole depending on the recipe. Okra can be cooked in many ways, such as braised, sautéed or baked. During cooking, it gives off a liquid that acts as a thickener. Serve okra as a side dish or mix it with other vegetables, meat or rice. It makes a nice addition to soups and stews.

stewed okra & shrimp

½ pound fresh okra
1 teaspoon canola or vegetable oil
½ cup finely chopped onion
1 can (about 14 ounces) no-salt-added
    stewed tomatoes, chopped,
    undrained
1 teaspoon dried thyme
¼ teaspoon salt
¾ cup fresh corn kernels or thawed
    frozen corn
½ teaspoon hot pepper sauce
2 ounces cooked baby shrimp

1. Remove and discard tip and stem ends from okra. Cut okra into ½-inch slices.

2. Heat oil in large nonstick skillet over medium heat. Add onion; cook and stir 3 minutes. Add okra; cook and stir 3 minutes. Add tomatoes, thyme and salt; bring to a boil over high heat. Reduce heat to low. Cover and simmer 10 minutes, stirring once.

3. Add corn and hot pepper sauce; cover and simmer 10 minutes. Stir in shrimp; cook and stir until heated through. *Makes 4 servings*

nutrients per serving:

Calories 107
Calories from Fat 14%
Protein 7g
Carbohydrate 19g
Fiber 3g

Total Fat 2g
Saturated Fat <1g
Cholesterol 28mg
Sodium 185mg

Dietary Exchanges:
Vegetable 2
Starch ½
Meat ½

Olive Oil

Olive oil should be a staple in your pantry. It's rich in heart-healthy fats, which are important for the many people with diabetes who also have heart disease.

benefits

Like all oils, olive oil contains a mix of saturated and unsaturated fats. Olive oil contains about 75 percent monounsaturated fat, making it one of the lowest of all oils in saturated fat, which raises levels of "bad" LDL cholesterol. Its high monounsaturated fat content has been shown to not only lower LDL levels when it replaces saturated fat in the diet but also help raise levels of "good" HDL cholesterol. In addition, extra virgin and virgin olive oils are rich in polyphenols, antioxidants that have strong heart-protective, anti-inflammatory action.

selection and storage

All types of olive oil contain the same calories and fat but differ in color, flavor and antioxidant content. Extra virgin and virgin olive oils have a greenish tint and are from the first pressing of the olives. Extra virgin olive oil is favored for its delicate flavor. Regular and light olive oils are more processed and lighter in color and flavor. Look for oils sold in dark bottles, which protect the oil from going rancid via oxidation caused by exposure to light. Store olive oil in a cool area and use within a few months to get the full benefits from its antioxidants.

preparation and serving tips

Due to its vast benefits, olive oil should be used in place of artery-clogging butter and margarine when cooking. Be careful when substituting olive oil in baking, as it will not work the same as butter or margarine.

nutrients per serving:

**Olive Oil
1 tablespoon**

Calories 119
Protein 0g
Total Fat 13.5g
Saturated Fat 2g

Monounsaturated Fat 10g
Cholesterol 0mg
Carbohydrate 0g
Dietary Fiber 0g
Sodium 0mg
Vitamin E 1.9mg
Iron 0.1mg

pasta with tuna, green beans & tomatoes

- 8 ounces uncooked whole wheat penne, rigatoni or fusilli pasta
- 1½ cups frozen cut green beans
- 3 teaspoons olive oil, divided
- 3 green onions, sliced
- 1 clove garlic, minced
- 1 can (about 14 ounces) diced Italian-style tomatoes, drained *or* 2 large tomatoes, chopped (about 2 cups)
- ½ teaspoon salt
- ½ teaspoon Italian seasoning
- ¼ teaspoon black pepper
- 1 can (12 ounces) solid albacore tuna packed in water, drained and flaked
- Chopped fresh parsley (optional)

1. Cook pasta according to package directions. Add green beans during last 7 minutes of cooking time (allow water to return to a boil before resuming timing). Drain and keep warm.

2. Meanwhile, heat 1 teaspoon oil in large skillet over medium heat. Add green onions and garlic; cook and stir 2 minutes. Add tomatoes, salt, Italian seasoning and pepper; cook and stir 4 to 5 minutes. Add pasta and green beans, tuna and remaining 2 teaspoons oil; mix gently. Garnish with parsley.

Makes 6 servings

nutrients per serving:

Calories 228
Calories from Fat 16%
Protein 15g
Carbohydrate 34g
Fiber 3g

Total Fat 4g
Saturated Fat <1g
Cholesterol 14mg
Sodium 345mg

Dietary Exchanges:
Vegetable 1
Starch 2
Meat 3

Onions

Along with garlic, shallots and leeks, onions are a member of the allium family and share many of the same health benefits, too. They can be used as a low-calorie flavorful ingredient in many dishes.

nutrients per serving:

Onion, white
½ cup raw chopped

Calories 32
Protein 1g
Total Fat 0g
Saturated Fat 0g
Cholesterol 0mg
Carbohydrate 8g
Dietary Fiber 1.5g
Sodium 0mg
Potassium 115mg
Calcium 18mg
Iron 0.2mg
Chromium 12mcg
Vitamin C 6mg
Folate 15mcg

benefits

Onions contain the mineral chromium, which plays a crucial role for people with diabetes by enhancing insulin's ability to lower blood sugar levels. Like their garlic cousins, onions appear useful in heart health by helping to lower blood cholesterol levels and reduce blood clotting. Additionally, onions contain phytonutrients that fight inflammation and improve the integrity of blood vessels. And green onions—with their brightly colored tops—provide vitamin A, which is essential for eye and skin health.

selection and storage

There are many varieties of onions that are found in various shapes and colors. Choose firm, dry onions with shiny, tissue-thin skins. Avoid those that are discolored or have wet spots. Onions keep three to four weeks in a dry, dark, cool location. Do not store them near potatoes, which give off a gas that causes onions to decay. Look for green onions with crisp, not wilted, tops; refrigerate them in an open plastic bag in the crisper drawer of the refrigerator.

preparation and serving tips

To minimize tears, refrigerate onions before cutting. Sweet, red and green onions are ideal raw; other onions are best cooked to mellow their flavor. Sauté or roast onions with a small amount of oil or broth. When using green onions, be sure to trim the roots and remove the outer layer before chopping.

oven-fried tex-mex onion rings

½ cup plain dry bread crumbs
⅓ cup yellow cornmeal
1½ teaspoons chili powder
⅛ teaspoon ground red pepper
⅛ teaspoon salt
1½ tablespoons butter, melted
1 teaspoon water
2 medium onions (about 10 ounces), sliced ½ inch thick
2 egg whites

1. Preheat oven to 450°F. Spray large nonstick baking sheet with nonstick cooking spray.

2. Combine bread crumbs, cornmeal, chili powder, ground red pepper and salt in medium shallow dish; mix well. Stir in butter and water.

3. Separate onion slices into rings. Place egg whites in large bowl; beat lightly. Dip onions; turn to coat. Transfer to bread crumb mixture; toss to coat. Place in single layer on prepared baking sheet.

4. Bake 12 to 15 minutes or until onions are tender and coating is crisp.   *Makes 6 servings*

nutrients per serving:

Calories 115
Calories from Fat 30%
Protein 4g
Carbohydrate 17g
Fiber 2g
Total Fat 4g
Saturated Fat 2g
Cholesterol 8mg
Sodium 165mg

Dietary Exchanges:
Starch 1
Fat 1

Oranges

In addition to providing soluble fiber to help with blood sugar control, oranges pack nutrients that battle diabetes complications. Plus, they have a sweet, tart flavor that makes them wonderful substitutes for high-calorie snacks and desserts.

benefits

This juicy fruit is best known for providing vitamin C to help prevent you from getting sick, but for people with diabetes the benefits go way beyond this. One orange provides 130 percent of the daily requirement for vitamin C, which helps control infections, maintain healthy teeth and gums and protect small blood vessels. Vitamin C, as an antioxidant, works with the folate and potassium found in oranges to slow the development of coronary heart disease. Additionally, vitamin C and the phytochemical beta-carotene support eye health and lower the risk of sight-stealing cataracts.

selection and storage

Oranges are one of the few fruits abundant in winter. California navels are the most popular oranges for eating on their own. The Valencias, grown in Florida, are the premier juice-producing oranges. Mandarin oranges are small and sweet with thin skins and easily sectioned segments and are also available canned. For all varieties, select firm fruit that are heavy for their size, indicating juiciness. Green color and blemishes are fine. Most varieties, except mandarins, will keep for two weeks in the refrigerator. Orange juice is available freshly squeezed or from or not from concentrate; just be sure it is 100 percent juice with no added sugar.

preparation and serving tips

For fruit salads or eating out of hand, choose seedless oranges. Top a spinach salad with orange segments. Try using orange juice to make marinades, sauces and dressings.

nutrients per serving:

Orange, navel 1 medium

Calories 69
Protein 1g
Total Fat 0g

Saturated Fat 0g
Cholesterol 0mg
Carbohydrate 18g
Dietary Fiber 3g
Sodium 0mg
Potassium 230mg

Calcium 60mg
Iron 0.2mg
Vitamin A 346 IU
Vitamin C 83mg
Folate 48mcg

marinated citrus shrimp

1 pound (about 32) large raw shrimp, peeled and deveined (with tails on), cooked
2 oranges, peeled and cut into segments
1 can (5½ ounces) pineapple chunks in juice, drained and ¼ cup juice reserved
2 green onions, sliced
½ cup orange juice
2 tablespoons minced fresh cilantro
2 tablespoons lime juice
2 tablespoons white wine vinegar
1 tablespoon olive or vegetable oil
1 clove garlic, minced
½ teaspoon dried basil
½ teaspoon dried tarragon
White pepper (optional)

1. Combine shrimp, oranges, pineapple and green onions in resealable food storage bag.

2. Whisk reserved pineapple juice, orange juice, cilantro, lime juice, vinegar, oil, garlic, basil, tarragon and white pepper, if desired, in medium bowl; pour over shrimp mixture. Seal bag; turn to coat. Marinate in refrigerator 2 hours or up to 8 hours.

Makes 16 servings

Oregano

Skip the salt and heavy sauces and sprinkle food with oregano to impart wonderful flavor. Of all the herbs, oregano has one of the highest antioxidant levels.

benefits

Beyond its role as a healthy flavor enhancer, oregano carries antioxidant nutrients that may give it even greater disease-fighting potential. Research into oregano's possible benefits is only in the preliminary stages but suggests the herb may help with blood sugar control as well as have positive effects on heart health and the integrity of blood vessels. Additionally, the lutein and zeaxanthin found in oregano may help prevent cataracts and certain other eye diseases.

selection and storage

Fresh oregano is often available in supermarkets; choose bright green, fresh-looking bunches free of wilting or yellowing. Refrigerate in a plastic bag for up to three days. Dried oregano is available in both crumbled and ground forms. It should be stored in a cool, dark place. For the best flavor and to get the maximum nutritional benefits, use dried oregano within six months.

preparation and serving tips

Oregano has an aromatic scent and robust taste. It goes extremely well with tomato-based dishes, such as pasta sauces, tomato soup and pizza. It also enhances cheese and egg dishes and can be used to add flavor to stews, soups and chilis. Oregano can be combined with other herbs and garlic to create a dry rub for meat. Fresh oregano is best used at the end of cooking or sprinkled on foods just before eating, whereas dried oregano can be added during cooking.

nutrients per serving:

**Oregano, dried
1 teaspoon**

Calories 3
Protein 0g
Total Fat 0g
Saturated Fat 0g
Cholesterol 0mg
Carbohydrate <1g
Dietary Fiber 0.5g
Sodium 0mg
Potassium 13mg
Calcium 16mg
Iron 0.4mg
Vitamin A 17 IU
Folate 2mcg

mediterranean chicken kabobs

2 pounds boneless skinless chicken
    breasts or chicken tenders, cut into
    1-inch pieces
1 small eggplant, peeled and cut into
    1-inch pieces
1 medium zucchini, cut crosswise into
    ½-inch slices
2 medium onions, each cut into 8 wedges
16 medium mushrooms, stems removed
16 cherry tomatoes
1 cup fat-free reduced-sodium chicken
    broth
⅔ cup balsamic vinegar
3 tablespoons olive oil
2 tablespoons dried mint
4 teaspoons dried basil
1 tablespoon dried oregano
2 teaspoons grated lemon peel
    Chopped fresh parsley (optional)
4 cups hot cooked couscous

1. Alternately thread chicken, eggplant, zucchini, onions, mushrooms and tomatoes onto 16 metal skewers; place in large glass baking dish.

2. Whisk broth, vinegar, oil, mint, basil and oregano in small bowl; pour over kabobs. Cover; marinate in refrigerator 2 hours, turning occasionally.

3. Preheat broiler. Remove kabobs from marinade; discard marinade. Broil kabobs 6 inches from heat source 10 to 15 minutes or until chicken is cooked through, turning kabobs halfway through cooking time.

4. Stir lemon peel and parsley, if desired, into couscous. Serve with kabobs.

Makes 8 servings

nutrients per serving:

Calories 300
Calories from Fat 16%
Protein 31g

Carbohydrate 32g
Fiber 4g
Total Fat 5g
Saturated Fat 1g
Cholesterol 69mg
Sodium 79mg

Dietary Exchanges:
Vegetable 3
Starch 1
Meat 3

Parsley

While this herb is most commonly used as a garnish, we shouldn't push it to the side of the plate. Parsley is rich in beneficial nutrients for people with diabetes.

benefits

Folk medicine suggests parsley as a treatment for diabetes. Animal studies have shown it has some ability to lower blood sugar, although further research is needed. Parsley does provide nutrients that can help ward off diabetes-related problems. It's rich in beta-carotene, vitamin C and flavonoids—all of which help protect against diabetes-related complications, including the inflammation and damage to blood vessels that can lead to heart attacks, strokes and vision loss.

selection and storage

Although there are several varieties, the most common forms of fresh parsley are curly-leaf and Italian flat-leaf. Choose parsley with bright green leaves free of wilting or yellowing. Store a bunch of parsley in a plastic bag in the refrigerator or place the stems in a cup of water, cover the tops loosely with plastic wrap and refrigerate for up to a week. Dried parsley is available in the spice section but does not have the same flavor as fresh.

preparation and serving tips

Fresh parsley should be rinsed well and patted dry. The leaves are often removed for chopping, but parts of the stem can also be used. Fresh parsley can be used in salads, such as tabbouleh, a Middle Eastern salad. Italian flat-leaf parsley is best used in cooked dishes, including soups, stews, stuffing, vegetable dishes, egg dishes, savory pies and casseroles; it can be cooked into a dish or sprinkled on top before serving.

nutrients per serving:

Parsley, fresh
¼ cup

Calories 5
Protein 0g

Total Fat 0g
Saturated Fat 0g
Cholesterol 0mg
Carbohydrate <1g
Dietary Fiber 0.5g
Sodium 10mg
Potassium 85mg

Calcium 21mg
Iron 0.9mg
Vitamin A 1,264 IU
Vitamin C 20mg
Folate 23mcg

low-carb tabbouleh

¼ cup uncooked bulgur
¼ cup water
¼ cup extra virgin olive oil
1 tablespoon lemon juice
1½ cups peeled, seeded and diced cucumbers
1½ cups diced tomatoes (3 medium tomatoes)
1 cup chopped fresh parsley
¼ cup chopped green onions
¼ cup chopped fresh mint leaves
2 teaspoons finely chopped walnuts
1 teaspoon chopped garlic
Salt to taste

1. Place bulgur in medium bowl; add water and let stand 15 minutes or until all liquid is absorbed.

2. Stir in oil and lemon juice. Add remaining ingredients. Cover and refrigerate at least 2 hours before serving, stirring occasionally.

Makes 6 servings

nutrients per serving:

Calories 125
Calories from Fat 68%
Protein 2g
Carbohydrate 9g
Fiber 2g
Total Fat 10g
Saturated Fat 1g
Cholesterol 0mg
Sodium 12mg

Dietary Exchanges:
Starch ½
Fat 2

Pasta

This comfort food no longer has to be banned from a diabetic diet. Whole wheat and whole grain pastas are a tasty way to enjoy this favorite fare without worrying about your blood sugar.

nutrients per serving:

Pasta, whole wheat
½ cup cooked

Calories 87
Protein 3.5g
Total Fat 0g
Saturated Fat 0g
Cholesterol 0mg
Carbohydrate 19g
Dietary Fiber 3g
Sodium 0mg
Potassium 30mg
Magnesium 21mg
Calcium 10mg
Iron 0.7mg
Vitamin A 2 IU
Folate 4mcg

benefits

Whole grain and whole wheat pastas are naturally rich in fiber, which slows the absorption of sugar, and in minerals, such as magnesium, that increase the body's sensitivity to insulin. This makes whole wheat or whole grain pasta a must, as these beneficial ingredients are typically lost or significantly reduced when grains are refined for white pasta. Additionally, newer varieties of healthy pastas, including products with added fiber, are especially helpful for diabetic diets.

selection and storage

To simplify your pasta choices, look for products labeled as whole wheat or whole grain. These are widely available in supermarkets and convenience stores.

Whole wheat pasta is darker in color and tends to have a chewier texture than white varieties. Whole grain pasta is made with a mix of nutrient-rich ingredients, including legumes, oats, barley and flax. Dried pasta will keep in your cupboard for several months.

preparation and serving tips

Whole wheat and whole grain pastas cook about the same as white—just follow package instructions to be sure. Pasta is best cooked until al dente—tender yet chewy. Drain immediately and do not rinse. To prevent sticking, immediately toss with olive oil or a low-fat vegetable sauce. For a meatless meal, toss whole wheat pasta with your favorite beans and vegetables, drizzle with olive oil and add a squeeze of lemon and some fresh herbs.

whole wheat penne with broccoli and sausage

6 ounces uncooked whole wheat penne pasta
8 ounces broccoli florets
8 ounces mild Italian turkey sausage, casings removed
1 medium onion, quartered and sliced
2 cloves garlic, minced
2 teaspoons grated lemon peel
¼ teaspoon salt
⅛ teaspoon black pepper
⅓ cup grated Parmesan cheese

1. Cook pasta according to package directions. Add broccoli during last 5 to 6 minutes of cooking time. Drain and keep warm.

2. Meanwhile, heat large nonstick skillet over medium heat. Crumble sausage into skillet. Add onion; cook until sausage is brown, stirring to break up meat. Drain fat. Add garlic; cook and stir 1 minute.

3. Add sausage mixture, lemon peel, salt and pepper to pasta and broccoli; toss well. Top each serving with Parmesan cheese.   *Makes 6 servings*

nutrients per serving:

Calories 208
Calories from Fat 27%
Protein 13g
Carbohydrate 26g
Fiber 4g
Total Fat 6g
Saturated Fat 1g
Cholesterol 26mg
Sodium 425mg

Dietary Exchanges:
Vegetable 1
Starch 1½
Meat 2
Fat 1

Pea Pods

Raw or cooked, snow peas and sugar snap peas are worthy of including in a diabetic diet. Their sweet taste and crunchy texture—along with their nutritional profile—make them a wonderful substitute for many carbohydrate-rich snacks.

benefits

Pea pods are low in calories and contain a mix of soluble and insoluble fibers, making them a good vegetable choice on multiple levels. The soluble fiber slows carbohydrate absorption, which helps to prevent blood sugar spikes. It's also a useful weapon against the elevated cholesterol levels so common among people with diabetes. The insoluble fiber provides a feeling of fullness. Snow peas and sugar snap peas also provide vitamin C and iron for immune health and potassium for blood pressure control.

selection and storage

Fresh snow peas (Chinese pea pods) are available year-round. Look for small, shiny, flat pods; they're the sweetest and most tender. Sugar snap peas have edible pods like snow peas but are sweet like green peas. Select those with plump, bright green pods. Many supermarkets sell prepackaged pea pods. When you can't get fresh pea pods, try frozen. They work wonderfully in cooking.

preparation and serving tips

Snow peas and sugar snap peas need washing and trimming before cooking or eating raw. If you're tired of the same old vegetables to snack on, try snap peas. Raw sugar snap peas go well with any low-fat dip. Sugar snap peas can also be lightly steamed and served as a side dish. Snow peas are the perfect addition to your favorite stir-fry; cook only a few minutes to keep them crisp.

nutrients per serving:

Peas, snow peas, sugar snap peas
½ cup raw

Calories 13
Protein 1g

Total Fat 0g
Saturated Fat 0g
Cholesterol 0mg
Carbohydrate 2.5g
Dietary Fiber 1g
Sodium 1.5mg

Potassium 63mg
Calcium 13.5mg
Iron 0.7mg
Vitamin A 343 IU
Vitamin C 18.9mg
Folate 13.3mcg

hot chinese chicken salad

8 ounces fresh or steamed Chinese egg noodles

¼ cup fat-free reduced-sodium chicken broth

2 tablespoons reduced-sodium soy sauce

2 tablespoons rice wine vinegar

1 tablespoon rice wine or dry sherry

1 teaspoon sugar

½ teaspoon red pepper flakes

3 teaspoons vegetable oil, divided

1½ cups fresh pea pods, diagonally sliced

1 cup thinly sliced green or red bell pepper

1 clove garlic, minced

1 pound boneless skinless chicken breasts, cut into ½-inch pieces

1 cup thinly sliced red or green cabbage

2 green onions, thinly sliced

1. Cook noodles in boiling water 4 to 5 minutes or until tender. Drain; set aside. Whisk broth, soy sauce, vinegar, rice wine, sugar and red pepper flakes in small bowl; set aside.

2. Heat 1 teaspoon oil in large nonstick skillet or wok over medium heat. Add pea pods, bell pepper and garlic; cook and stir 2 minutes or until vegetables are crisp-tender. Remove from skillet; set aside.

3. Heat remaining 2 teaspoons oil in skillet. Add chicken; cook and stir 3 to 4 minutes or until cooked through. Add cabbage, cooked vegetables and noodles. Stir in sauce; cook and stir 1 to 2 minutes or until heated through. Sprinkle with green onions before serving.   *Makes 6 servings*

nutrients per serving:

Calories 241
Calories from Fat 14%
Protein 23g
Carbohydrate 27g

Fiber 3g
Total Fat 4g
Saturated Fat 1g
Cholesterol 45mg
Sodium 419mg

Dietary Exchanges:
Vegetable 1
Starch 1½
Meat 2

Peaches

In China, the peach symbolizes a long life. Perhaps that's because fresh peaches are a good source of an array of nutrients.

benefits

Fresh peaches are a low-calorie source of beta-carotene and vitamin C, antioxidant nutrients that researchers believe may help prevent complications of diabetes, such as nerve damage and eye disease. Peaches also supply soluble fiber that helps prevent spikes in blood sugar levels.

nutrients per serving:

**Peach
1 medium**

Calories 58
Protein 1g
Total Fat 0g
Saturated Fat 0g
Cholesterol 0mg
Carbohydrate 14g
Dietary Fiber 2g
Sodium 0mg
Potassium 285mg
Calcium 9mg
Iron 0.4mg
Vitamin A 489 IU
Vitamin C 10mg
Folate 6mcg

selection and storage

Peaches are at their best in late summer. A fresh peach has velvety skin that can range from golden red to creamy pink and flesh that is bright orange to creamy white. Look for fragrant fruit that gives slightly to pressure. Be cautious of soft spots, as peaches bruise easily. Place peaches in a paper bag with an apple to speed up the ripening process. Once ripe, they will last in the refrigerator for up to five days. When fresh peaches aren't available, try frozen, canned or dried peaches. To keep calories low, look for canned peaches in water or juice and frozen or dried peaches without added sugar.

preparation and serving tips

Rinse fresh peaches and eat with the peel for more fiber. Peaches can be enjoyed as a light snack or in fruit salads, salsas and smoothies. They can be mixed with low-fat cottage cheese for a light breakfast. For a fun summer meal, try grilling or broiling fresh peach halves on a kabob with your favorite meat or poultry. Just season peaches with a touch of cinnamon or nutmeg to get a sweet, smoky flavor.

peaches with raspberry sauce

1 cup raspberries
½ cup water
¼ cup measure-for-measure sugar
   substitute
6 peach halves
⅓ cup vanilla nonfat yogurt

1. Combine raspberries, water and sugar substitute in small saucepan; bring to a boil over medium-high heat, stirring frequently. Boil 1 minute. Transfer to food processor or blender; process until smooth. Let stand 15 minutes to cool.

2. Drizzle ¼ cup raspberry sauce onto each of six serving dishes. Place one peach half on each dish. Spoon about 2½ teaspoons yogurt over each peach half.   *Makes 6 servings*

nutrients per serving:

Calories 41
Calories from Fat 0%
Protein 1g
Carbohydrate 10g
Fiber 2g
Total Fat 0g
Saturated Fat 0g
Cholesterol <1mg
Sodium 9mg

Dietary Exchanges:
Fruit ½

Peanuts

Because they are rich in protein, peanuts and peanut butter are great in any diet. They provide long-lasting energy and essential heart-protective nutrients with little effect on blood sugar.

benefits

The combination of protein, fiber and fat found in peanuts means they digest more slowly and provide fuel over time without causing blood sugar spikes. They also have a vast amount of benefits on heart health. Peanuts are rich in monounsaturated fats, which help lower LDL, or "bad," cholesterol; niacin, which helps raise levels of HDL, or "good," cholesterol; and potassium for blood pressure control. Additionally, they contain a high amount of magnesium, a mineral that is often found in low levels in people with diabetes.

selection and storage

Peanuts are sold shelled or unshelled. When buying in the shell, look for clean, unbroken shells that do not rattle when shaken. Shelled peanuts, available in vacuum-sealed containers, are usually roasted and often salted. Choose dry roasted peanuts rather than oil roasted for less fat and calories. Unshelled nuts can keep for a few months in a cool, dry location. Once they're shelled or the container has been opened, they should be stored in the refrigerator or freezer for up to three months. Peanut butter is available as natural or blended and may contain added sugar.

preparation and serving tips

Enjoy peanuts as a snack, but keep your portion to about 1 ounce, or a small handful. Sprinkle peanuts on salads or stir-fries for added crunch and flavor. Peanut butter has many uses besides sandwiches. Enjoy it for a snack spread on apple wedges, crackers or toast.

nutrients per serving:

**Peanuts, dry roasted without salt
1 ounce**

Calories 166
Protein 7g
Total Fat 14g
Saturated Fat 2g
Cholesterol 0mg
Carbohydrate 6g
Dietary Fiber 2.5g
Sodium 0mg
Potassium 185mg
Magnesium 50mg
Phosphorus 101mg
Calcium 15mg
Iron 0.6mg
Folate 41mcg
Niacin 3.8mg
Vitamin E 2mg

Pears

The juicy flavor and crisp bite of pears make them a delightful fruit to munch on. Plus, they are filled with fiber to help keep blood sugar levels even.

benefits

You can't pick a fruit that outpaces pears in fiber. Pears' soluble fiber helps keep blood sugar in a more desirable range, likely decreasing the risk of diabetes-related complications. It also helps protect the more fragile diabetic heart and blood vessels by decreasing the "bad" LDL cholesterol that can contribute to hardening of the arteries, which in turn can foster heart attacks and strokes. Pears provide heart-healthy potassium, vitamin C and folate, too.

selection and storage

The juicy fresh Bartletts are the most common variety and are also available canned. The Anjous, which are firmer and not quite as sweet, are all-purpose pears. So are the Boscs, which have elongated necks and unusual russet coloring. Bosc pears are crunchy, while Comice pears are the sweetest. Pears ripen from the inside out, so it's best to buy them firm but not rock hard. Ripen them on the counter or in a ventilated paper bag, but do not pile them up or they'll bruise. Canned pears have more calories when packed in syrup and less fiber because the skins have been removed.

preparation and serving tips

To get a pear's full nutritional value, be sure to eat the skin. Firm pears work well in salads or for cooking. Ripe pears are great mixed with nonfat yogurt and cereal for breakfast. Bartlett and Bosc pears are good for cooking.

nutrients per serving:

Pear
1 medium

Calories 103
Protein 1g
Total Fat 0g

Saturated Fat 0g
Cholesterol 0mg
Carbohydrate 28g
Dietary Fiber 5.5g
Sodium 0mg
Potassium 210mg

Calcium 16mg
Iron 0.3mg
Vitamin A 41 IU
Vitamin C 8mg
Folate 12mcg

Pecans

Whether you call them "pee-canz" or "pa-kawnz," these versatile, rich-tasting nuts offer nutrients that can help protect you from diabetes-related damage.

nutrients per serving:

Pecans, dry roasted without salt
1 ounce

Calories 201
Protein 3g
Total Fat 21g
Saturated Fat 2g
Cholesterol 0mg
Carbohydrate 4g
Dietary Fiber 2.5g
Sodium 0mg
Potassium 120mg
Phosphorus 83mg
Calcium 20mg
Iron 0.8mg
Zinc 1.4mg
Magnesium 37mg
Vitamin A 40 IU
Vitamin E 0.4mg

benefits

Just a handful of pecans contains a lot of nutrients that can help protect you from certain diabetes-related conditions, especially heart disease. Studies have shown that including just a few ounces of pecans daily in a heart-healthy diet can reduce damaging triglyceride and LDL cholesterol levels while increasing protective HDL cholesterol levels. Pecans contain vitamin E, which helps prevent damage to the heart and blood vessels, as well as potassium, calcium and magnesium, minerals that help to lower blood pressure. And a single serving, about 19 halves, provides about 10 percent of the daily requirement of fiber, which is also associated with a lower risk of heart disease.

selection and storage

Shelled pecans are available as halves, chips or ground. They may be raw, dry or oil roasted and salted or unsalted. Unsalted raw pecans are usually used in recipes, while roasted varieties are best for snacking.

Choose unsalted dry roasted pecans for fewer calories and less sodium. Check the freshness date on packaged pecans. Shelled pecans will keep up to nine months in the refrigerator, or they can be stored for three months in a cool, dry place. Unshelled pecans will keep for three to six months in a cool, dry place.

preparation and serving tips

Use pecans to top salads, vegetables and cereal. They add flavor and crunch to cookies, muffins and other baked goods. Try breading chicken or fish with ground pecans for a lower-carbohydrate dinner.

choco-coco pecan crisps

1 cup packed light brown sugar
½ cup (1 stick) butter, softened
1 egg
1 teaspoon vanilla
1½ cups all-purpose flour
1 cup chopped pecans
⅓ cup unsweetened cocoa powder
½ teaspoon baking soda
1 cup flaked coconut

1. Beat brown sugar and butter in large bowl with electric mixer at medium speed until light and fluffy. Beat in egg and vanilla.

2. Combine flour, pecans, cocoa and baking soda in small bowl; mix well. Add to butter mixture; beat until stiff dough is formed.

3. Sprinkle coconut on work surface. Divide dough into four parts. Shape each part into log about 1½ inches in diameter; roll in coconut until thickly coated. Wrap in plastic wrap; refrigerate 1 hour or until firm.

4. Preheat oven to 350°F. Cut rolls into ⅛-inch-thick slices. Place 2 inches apart on ungreased cookie sheets. Bake 10 to 13 minutes or until firm but not overly browned. Remove to wire racks to cool completely. *Makes 72 servings*

nutrients per serving:

Calories 50
Calories from Fat 50%
Protein 1g
Carbohydrate 6g
Fiber 0g

Total Fat 3g
Saturated Fat 2g
Cholesterol 5mg
Sodium 15mg

Dietary Exchanges:
Starch ½
Fat ½

Pineapple

Pineapple gets high scores for its exceptionally sweet and tart taste and health-protective nutrients. It's a great way to satisfy your sweet tooth, too.

benefits

Pineapple provides more than a third of the daily recommended allowance of vitamin C, an antioxidant that helps with immune health. This is important for people with diabetes because they are at greater risk for infections. Vitamin C is also a powerful antioxidant that helps protect against heart disease. Pineapple also offers heart-protective folate and potassium, which are needed for healthy blood pressure.

selection and storage

When choosing pineapple, let your nose be your guide. A ripe pineapple gives off a sweet aroma from its base. Color is not a reliable indicator; ripe pineapples vary in color by variety. Choose a large pineapple that feels heavy for its size, indicating juiciness and a lot of pulp. A ripe pineapple yields slightly when pressed. Once a pineapple is picked, it will not ripen further. Canned pineapple is available; be sure to select varieties packed in juice or water, not syrup.

preparation and serving tips

Preparing a pineapple is not as scary as it looks. Cut off the bottom and top, then peel the outside using a sharp knife. Remove any remaining eyes. Cut into quarters and remove the core from each quarter, then cut into slices. Use pineapple in fruit salads or make fruit kabobs for a unique dessert. Pineapple works well when grilled; try it alone or on a kabob with your favorite meat.

nutrients per serving:

Pineapple ½ cup raw

Calories 41
Protein 1g
Total Fat 0g

Saturated Fat 0g
Cholesterol 0mg
Carbohydrate 11g
Dietary Fiber 1g
Sodium 0mg
Potassium 90mg

Calcium 11mg
Iron 0.2mg
Manganese 0.8mg
Vitamin C 39mg
Folate 15mcg

banana-pineapple breakfast shake

- 2 cups plain nonfat yogurt
- 1 can (8 ounces) crushed pineapple in juice, undrained
- 1 cup ice cubes
- 1 ripe medium banana
- 8 packets sugar substitute
- 1 teaspoon vanilla
- ⅛ teaspoon ground nutmeg

Combine yogurt, pineapple, ice, banana, sugar substitute, vanilla and nutmeg in blender; blend until smooth. Serve immediately.

Makes 4 servings

nutrients per serving:

Calories 140
Calories from Fat 2%
Protein 8g
Carbohydrate 27g
Fiber 1g
Total Fat <1g
Saturated Fat <1g
Cholesterol 2mg
Sodium 95mg

Dietary Exchanges:
Fruit 1½
Milk ½

Pistachios

Compared to other popular nuts, pistachios are among the highest in protein and fiber and one of the lowest in calories and fat. They also offer loads of key nutrients.

benefits

Pistachios are useful for the many people with diabetes who also have heart disease. These yummy green nuts are full of phytosterols, natural compounds that compete with cholesterol for absorption by the body, helping reduce blood cholesterol levels. They also contain arginine, an amino acid that helps improve circulation. Pistachios are rich in monounsaturated fats, the same heart-healthy fats found in olive oil. And they provide a hefty amount of resveratrol, a phytonutrient (also found in wine) that may play a role in fighting heart disease and cancer. Additionally, pistachios offer noteworthy amounts of potassium, magnesium and vitamin E.

selection and storage

Pistachios are increasingly available shelled but are more expensive than the commonly found unshelled form. They are available either raw or roasted and salted or unsalted. When buying unshelled pistachios, the shells should be partly opened, which not only makes it easier to remove the nut but also indicates that the nut is mature and ready to be eaten. Store pistachios in an airtight container in the refrigerator for up to three months or in the freezer for up to one year.

preparation and serving tips

Pistachios work well in savory or sweet dishes. They can be toasted and added to vegetable or rice dishes. Or sprinkle a handful of chopped pistachios on breakfast cereal or salads for an extra crunch. Swap them out with walnuts that are traditionally used in baking; try using them in muffins, cakes or cookies.

nutrients per serving:

Pistachios, dry roasted without salt 1 ounce

Calories 161
Protein 6g
Total Fat 13g
Saturated Fat 1.5g
Cholesterol 0mg
Carbohydrate 8g
Dietary Fiber 3g
Sodium 0mg
Potassium 285mg
Calcium 30mg
Iron 1.1mg
Vitamin A 73 IU
Vitamin C 1mg
Folate 14mcg
Magnesium 31mg
Vitamin E 0.7mg

pistachio pinwheels

1 package (8 ounces) reduced-fat
   cream cheese, softened
½ cup (1 stick) soft baking butter with
   canola oil
2 cups all-purpose flour
3 tablespoons apricot fruit spread
1 tablespoon water
2 tablespoons sugar
¼ teaspoon ground cinnamon
½ cup finely chopped pistachios,
   toasted*
   Nonstick cooking spray

*To toast nuts, spread in single layer on baking
sheet. Bake in preheated 350°F oven 5 to 7 minutes
or until golden brown, stirring frequently.

1. Preheat oven to 350°F. Line cookie sheets
with parchment paper.

2. Beat cream cheese in large bowl with
electric mixer at low speed 30 seconds or
until smooth. Beat in butter. Add flour in
three batches, beating after each addition
until blended. Divide dough into two equal
portions; shape into rectangles. Wrap in
plastic wrap; refrigerate 20 minutes.

3. Whisk fruit spread and water in small bowl.
Combine sugar and cinnamon in another
small bowl.

4. Roll out each piece of dough into
12×10-inch rectangle on lightly floured
surface. Spread 2 tablespoons apricot mixture
onto each rectangle. Sprinkle each with
1½ teaspoons sugar-cinnamon mixture and
¼ cup pistachios. Cut each dough rectangle
in half lengthwise into two 12×5-inch pieces.
Roll up each piece jelly-roll style, starting
with long side.

5. Cut each roll into 16 slices. Place on
prepared cookie sheets. Spray tops of cookies
with cooking spray; sprinkle evenly with
remaining sugar-cinnamon mixture.

6. Bake 16 minutes or until golden. Cool on
cookie sheets 2 minutes. Remove to wire
racks to cool completely.

Makes 64 servings

nutrients per serving:

Calories 45
Calories from Fat 60%
Protein 1g
Carbohydrate 5g
Fiber <1g
Total Fat 3g
Saturated Fat <1g
Cholesterol 3mg
Sodium 34mg

Dietary Exchanges:
Starch ½
Fat ½

Plums

You can't go wrong with this juicy fruit. Considering their small size, plums provide quite a hefty amount of nutrients. And what makes them even greater is how versatile they are in cooking.

nutrients per serving:

Plum
1 medium

Calories 30
Protein <1g
Total Fat 0g
Saturated Fat 0g
Cholesterol 0mg
Carbohydrate 7g
Dietary Fiber 1g
Sodium 0mg
Potassium 105mg
Calcium 4mg
Iron 0.1mg
Vitamin A 228 IU
Vitamin C 6mg
Folate 3mcg

benefits

Plums provide minimal calories and a generous dose of vitamins A and C, potassium and fiber—nutrients that provide protection against diabetes-related complications, including damage to the blood vessels, which can lead to infections. Dried plums, or prunes, are especially beneficial for diabetes, as they're a concentrated source of soluble fiber, which helps increase insulin sensitivity and stabilize blood sugar levels after a meal.

selection and storage

Plums are a summer fruit with a long season from May through October. Some plums cling to their pits while others have "free" stones (pits). Plum skins come in a rainbow of colors: red, purple, black, green, blue and even yellow. The flesh varies, too, and can be yellow, orange, green or red.

Look for plump fruit with a bright or deep color. If they yield to gentle palm pressure, they're ripe. Once slightly soft, they should be eaten or refrigerated.

preparation and serving tips

Like many fruits, plums taste sweetest when they're at room temperature. Plums can be added to fruit salads, baked goods, compotes, puddings or meat dishes. They can also be made into butters, jams, purées or sauces. Puréed dried plums (prunes) make a fabulous fat substitute in recipes for quick breads, muffins and other baked goods. Not only do they substantially reduce calories, they also boost the nutrition content.

glazed plum pastry

1 package (about 17 ounces) frozen puff
    pastry sheets, thawed
3 tablespoons sucralose-sugar blend,
    divided
2 tablespoons all-purpose flour
8 plums (about 2 pounds)
¼ teaspoon ground cinnamon
⅓ cup sugar-free apricot preserves

1. Preheat oven to 400°F. Line 18×12-inch baking sheet with parchment paper.

2. Unfold pastry sheets on prepared baking sheet. Place pastry sheets side by side so fold lines are parallel to length of baking sheet and so they overlap ½ inch in center. Press center seam firmly to seal. Trim ends to fit baking sheet. Prick entire surface with fork.

3. Combine 2 tablespoons sucralose-sugar blend and flour in small bowl. Sprinkle evenly over pastry to within ½ inch of edges. Bake 12 to 15 minutes or until pastry is slightly puffed and golden.

4. Cut plums in half lengthwise; remove pits. Cut crosswise into ⅛-inch-thick slices. Arrange slices slightly overlapping in five rows down length of pastry.

5. Combine remaining 1 tablespoon sucralose-sugar blend and cinnamon in small bowl; sprinkle evenly over plums. Bake 15 minutes or until plums are tender and pastry is browned. Remove to wire rack.

6. Place preserves in small microwavable bowl. Microwave on HIGH 30 to 40 seconds or until melted. Brush preserves over plums. Cool 10 to 15 minutes before serving.

Makes 20 servings

nutrients per serving:

Calories 152
Calories from Fat 47%
Protein 2g
Carbohydrate 18g
Fiber 1g

Total Fat 8g
Saturated Fat 2g
Cholesterol 0mg
Sodium 53mg

Dietary Exchanges:
Starch 1

Pork Tenderloin

Chicken no longer has to be the center of your plate. Pork tenderloin is lean and rich in plenty of nutrients, making it a great substitute for the poultry you may be getting tired of.

benefits

Pork tenderloin is comparable to skinless chicken breast in calories, total fat and saturated fat. It is also lower in cholesterol, so it's a good fit for a heart-healthy diabetes diet. Its high quality protein leaves you feeling satisfied, which will help in any weight-loss efforts. Pork tenderloin also provides more than 20 percent of your daily requirements for many B vitamins, including thiamin, niacin, riboflavin and vitamin B_6, as well as the mineral phosphorus. This is important because the body needs B vitamins to turn food into energy.

selection and storage

Pork tenderloin is long and thin and easy to find in the fresh meat section of the supermarket. About 4 ounces raw will yield a 3-ounce cooked serving. Prepackaged fresh pork tenderloin can be stored in the refrigerator for up to four days; well-wrapped, it can be stored in the freezer for up to six months.

preparation and serving tips

Pork tenderloin makes an elegant entrée for a dinner party but can also easily be roasted or grilled for a quick meal. It has a mild flavor, so it's best when prepared with a spice rub, marinade, stuffing or flavorful sauce. To keep the tenderloin juicy, be careful not to overcook it. A meat thermometer inserted into the thickest part of the meat should reach a temperature of 160°F for medium doneness.

nutrients per serving:

**Pork Tenderloin
3 ounces roasted**

Calories 125
Protein 22g
Total Fat 3.5g
Saturated Fat 1g
Cholesterol 62mg
Carbohydrate <1g
Dietary Fiber 0g
Sodium 50mg
Potassium 355mg
Thiamin 0.8mg
Riboflavin 0.3mg
Niacin 6.3mg
Vitamin B₆ 0.6mg
Phosphorus 225mg

easy moo shu pork

7 ounces pork tenderloin
  Olive oil cooking spray
4 green onions, cut into ½-inch pieces
1½ cups packaged coleslaw mix
2 tablespoons hoisin sauce or Asian plum sauce
4 (8-inch) fat-free flour tortillas, warmed

1. Thinly slice pork. Spray large nonstick skillet with cooking spray; heat over medium-high heat. Add pork and green onions; cook and stir 2 to 3 minutes or until pork is cooked through. Stir in coleslaw mix and hoisin sauce.

2. Spoon pork mixture onto tortillas; wrap to enclose filling. Serve immediately.

Makes 2 servings

Note: To warm tortillas, stack and wrap loosely in plastic wrap. Microwave on HIGH for 15 to 20 seconds.

nutrients per serving:

Calories 293
Calories from Fat 13%
Protein 26g
Carbohydrate 37g
Fiber 14g
Total Fat 4g
Saturated Fat 1g
Cholesterol 58mg
Sodium 672mg

Dietary Exchanges:
Vegetable 1
Starch 2
Meat 2

Potatoes

While potatoes may seem like they belong on the "bad" food list for your diabetic diet, they don't. They are packed with nutrients that can actually help you manage your disease.

nutrients per serving:

Potato
1 medium baked

Calories 161
Protein 4g
Total Fat 0g
Saturated Fat 0g
Cholesterol 0mg
Carbohydrate 37g
Dietary Fiber 4g
Sodium 15mg
Potassium 925mg
Calcium 26mg
Iron 1.9mg
Vitamin A 17 IU
Vitamin C 17mg
Folate 48mcg

benefits

Potatoes are packed with heart-protective, immune-boosting vitamin C and blood pressure-lowering potassium. They're rather filling and yet free of fat and cholesterol. While they are high in carbohydrates, you can make them more diabetes friendly by leaving the peel on. Eating the potato with its skin on provides a richer dose of fiber to help slow digestion. Because some of the fiber is soluble, it also limits the rise in blood sugar and helps lower blood cholesterol. Forgo any fatty, high-calorie toppings and deep-frying, too.

selection and storage

There are hundreds of varieties of potatoes. Many are all-purpose, but russets are best for baking while new potatoes are suited for boiling. Choose potatoes that are firm with no soft or dark spots. Store potatoes in a dry, cool, dark, ventilated location, away from onions. Mature potatoes keep for several weeks; new potatoes keep for only one week.

preparation and serving tips

Just before cooking, scrub potatoes well with a vegetable brush and cut out sprout buds and bad spots. Prick the skin for a fluffier potato. Baking a potato takes 1 hour in the oven but only 5 minutes in the microwave. Try a healthy version of a loaded baked potato: Top with nonfat yogurt and sprinkle with chopped dill or scallions. For a French fry fix, toss thin-cut potatoes with olive oil and season with salt and pepper; roast in a 400°F oven for about 30 minutes.

retro beef and veggie soup stew

3 teaspoons olive oil, divided
¾ pound beef top sirloin steak, cut into
    bite-size pieces
2 medium carrots, quartered lengthwise
    and cut into 2-inch pieces
1 medium green bell pepper, coarsely
    chopped
6 ounces green beans, cut into 2-inch pieces
1 can (about 14 ounces) Italian-style
    stewed tomatoes
1 cup beef broth
8 ounces new potatoes, cut into
    bite-size pieces
3 teaspoons instant coffee granules,
    divided
2 tablespoons all-purpose flour
¾ teaspoon salt
¼ teaspoon black pepper

1. Heat 1 teaspoon oil in Dutch oven over medium-high heat. Brown beef 1 to 2 minutes. Remove from skillet; set aside.

2. Add remaining 2 teaspoons oil, carrots, bell pepper and green beans to Dutch oven. Cook and stir 4 minutes or until edges begin to brown. Add tomatoes, broth, potatoes and 1 teaspoon coffee; bring to a boil. Reduce heat to low. Add beef; cover and simmer 20 minutes or until potatoes are tender.

3. Stir in remaining 2 teaspoons coffee, flour, salt and black pepper. Cook, uncovered, 10 to 15 minutes or until thickened.

Makes 4 servings

nutrients per serving:

Calories 265
Calories from Fat 23%
Protein 23g
Carbohydrate 28g
Fiber 5g
Total Fat 7g
Saturated Fat 2g
Cholesterol 31mg
Sodium 589mg

Dietary Exchanges:
Starch 2
Meat 2

Pumpkin Seeds

Like nuts and other seeds, pumpkin seeds and pepitas (hulled pumpkin seeds) are rich in protein, fiber and unsaturated fats, making them great for a diabetic diet.

nutrients per serving:

Pumpkin Seeds, unhulled, dry roasted without salt
½ ounce

Calories 63
Protein 3g
Total Fat 3g
Saturated Fat 0.5g
Cholesterol 0mg
Carbohydrate 8g
Dietary Fiber 2.5g
Sodium 0mg
Potassium 130mg
Calcium 8mg
Iron 0.5mg
Vitamin A 9 IU
Folate 1mcg
Magnesium 37mg

benefits

Because of their fat, protein and fiber contents, pumpkin seeds can help stabilize blood sugar levels. The fat they contain is mostly monounsaturated and omega-3 polyunsaturated, which help lower total and "bad" LDL cholesterol and raise beneficial HDL cholesterol. A diet rich in these fats is associated with a lower risk of coronary heart disease, a common diabetes-related condition. Pumpkin seeds also offer potassium and magnesium, which help lower blood pressure.

selection and storage

Pumpkin seeds can be purchased with or without the white hull, roasted or raw and with or without salt. Dry roasted pumpkin seeds without salt are the healthiest option. Pale green pepitas are often sold roasted and salted but may also be available raw or unsalted. They can be found in the Mexican food section of the supermarket. Pumpkin seeds will keep in an airtight container in a cool, dark place for several months.

preparation and serving tips

To roast pumpkin seeds, scoop them out of the pumpkin, rinse them and let dry. Bake them on a greased baking sheet at 350°F for 20 minutes or until crisp. Lightly salt them while warm, if desired. Enjoy them as a crunchy snack or combine them with nuts, dried fruits and cereals for a fun trail mix. Pepitas are a popular ingredient in Mexican cooking and can be sprinkled on salads or baked into breads and cookies.

southwest snack mix

4 cups unsweetened corn cereal squares
2 cups unsalted pretzels
½ cup unsalted pumpkin seeds
1½ teaspoons chili powder
1 teaspoon minced fresh cilantro or parsley
½ teaspoon garlic powder
½ teaspoon onion powder
1 egg white
2 tablespoons olive oil
2 tablespoons lime juice

1. Preheat oven to 300°F. Spray baking sheet with nonstick cooking spray.

2. Combine cereal, pretzels and pumpkin seeds in large bowl. Combine chili powder, cilantro, garlic powder and onion powder in small bowl.

3. Whisk egg white, oil and lime juice in small bowl until well blended. Pour over cereal mixture; toss to coat. Add seasoning mixture; toss lightly to coat. Transfer to prepared baking sheet.

4. Bake 45 minutes, stirring every 15 minutes. Cool completely. Store in airtight container.

Makes 12 servings

nutrients per serving:

Calories 93
Calories from Fat 28%
Protein 2g

Carbohydrate 15g
Fiber 1g
Total Fat 3g
Saturated Fat <1g
Cholesterol 0mg

Sodium 114mg

Dietary Exchanges:
Starch 1
Fat ½

Quinoa

With more protein and fiber than most grains, quinoa makes a great addition to a diabetic meal plan.

benefits

Quinoa contains fewer carbohydrates and more protein than rice and other grains do, making it less likely to cause blood sugar spikes. Quinoa's protein content is similar to that of meat and other animal products, so it's quite filling; yet it has the added benefit of heart-healthy unsaturated fats rather than the saturated fats found in meat and dairy. Quinoa is rich in phytonutrients that help protect against cardiovascular disease and other diabetes-related conditions. And its fiber, magnesium and vitamin E contents may help improve insulin sensitivity.

nutrients per serving:

Quinoa
½ cup cooked

Calories 111
Protein 4g
Total Fat 2g
Saturated Fat 0g
Cholesterol 0mg
Carbohydrate 20g
Dietary Fiber 2.5g
Sodium 6mg
Potassium 160mg
Iron 1.4mg
Zinc 1mg
Magnesium 59mg
Phosphorus 141mg
Folate 39mcg
Vitamin E 0.6mg

selection and storage

Quinoa is becoming more popular and is now available in many supermarkets near the rice and other grains. It has a tiny beaded shape and may be available as red, black or ivory-colored. Quinoa should be stored in a sealed container in a cool, dry place or in the refrigerator. Quinoa is also available ground into flour and in several forms of pasta.

preparation and serving tips

Rinse quinoa in a fine-mesh sieve before cooking. Combine one part quinoa to two parts water or broth in a medium or large saucepan. (Allow for room since it will expand to four times its original volume when it's cooked.) Bring to a simmer and reduce the heat to low. Cover and cook for about 15 minutes or until quinoa is tender and the water is absorbed. Quinoa has a delicate flavor and can be substituted for other grains in almost any recipe. While great on its own, it works well in any dish from soups, salads and side dishes to hot breakfast cereal.

quinoa & mango salad

1 cup uncooked quinoa
2 cups water
2 cups cubed peeled mangoes (about
2 large mangoes)
½ cup sliced green onions
½ cup dried cranberries
2 tablespoons chopped fresh parsley
¼ cup olive oil
1 tablespoon plus 1½ teaspoons white
wine vinegar
1 teaspoon Dijon mustard
½ teaspoon salt
⅛ teaspoon black pepper

1. Place quinoa in fine-mesh strainer; rinse well. Transfer to medium saucepan and add water. Bring to a boil. Reduce heat; cover and simmer about 15 minutes or until all water is absorbed. Let stand 15 minutes. Transfer to large bowl; cover and refrigerate at least 1 hour.

2. Add mangoes, green onions, cranberries and parsley; mix well.

3. Whisk oil, vinegar, mustard, salt and pepper in small bowl until blended. Pour over quinoa mixture; toss to coat. _Makes 8 servings_

Tip: This salad can be made several hours ahead and refrigerated. Allow it to stand at room temperature for at least 30 minutes before serving.

nutrients per serving:

Calories 200
Calories from Fat 37%
Protein 3g
Carbohydrate 30g
Fiber 3g
Total Fat 8g
Saturated Fat 1g
Cholesterol 0mg
Sodium 172mg

Dietary Exchanges:
Fruit 1
Starch 1
Fat 1½

Raspberries

These sweet, juicy berries pack fabulous flavor and some serious punch when it comes to helping you fend off diabetes complications. Raspberries are almost unrivaled in their nutrient content.

benefits

Raspberries are great for any diet; they are low in calories and provide a whopping 8 grams of fiber per cup. They're high in pectin, a soluble fiber that helps steady blood sugar levels as well as lower blood cholesterol, which is often elevated in people with diabetes. Among raspberries' phytonutrients are anthocyanins, which have been found to help reduce blood sugar after a carbohydrate-rich meal. Additionally, raspberries contain an appreciable amount of vitamin C, an antioxidant that offers immune protection, which is helpful for people with diabetes who are at greater risk for infections.

selection and storage

Raspberries are fragile and should be handled carefully and eaten soon after purchasing. Look for berries that are brightly colored with no hulls attached. Avoid any that look shriveled or have visible mold. They should be plump, firm and packed in a shallow container and have a clean, slightly sweet fragrance. Frozen unsweetened raspberries are also an option and work well in smoothies and baked goods.

preparation and serving tips

Rinse raspberries under cool water just before serving. Purée fresh or frozen raspberries to create a sweet and tart sauce to top a fruit salad. If you're celebrating a special occasion, enjoy a glass of champagne with some chilled raspberries. Raspberries also make a colorful garnish.

nutrients per serving:

Raspberries
½ cup

Calories 32
Protein 1g
Total Fat 0g
Saturated Fat 0g
Cholesterol 0mg
Carbohydrate 7g
Dietary Fiber 4g
Sodium 0mg
Potassium 95mg
Calcium 15mg
Iron 0.4mg
Vitamin A 20 IU
Vitamin C 16mg
Folate 13mcg

apple-raspberry granola skillet

1 cup low-fat granola without raisins
2 tablespoons water
1 tablespoon lemon juice
2 teaspoons cornstarch
1 pound apples, cored and sliced
½ teaspoon ground cinnamon
4 ounces fresh raspberries
3 packets sugar substitute
½ teaspoon vanilla
¼ teaspoon almond extract

1. Place granola in small resealable food storage bag; seal tightly. Crush to coarse crumbs; set aside.

2. Whisk water, lemon juice and cornstarch in small bowl until cornstarch is completely dissolved.

3. Heat large nonstick skillet over medium-high heat. Add apples, cornstarch mixture and cinnamon; stir until blended. Bring to a boil. Boil 1 minute or until thickened, stirring constantly.

4. Remove skillet from heat. Gently stir in raspberries, sugar substitute, vanilla and almond extract. Sprinkle granola crumbs over top. Let stand, uncovered, 30 minutes before serving. *Makes 8 servings*

nutrients per serving:

Calories 90
Calories from Fat 10%
Protein 1g
Carbohydrate 21g
Fiber 3g

Total Fat 1g
Saturated Fat 0g
Cholesterol 0mg
Sodium 25mg

Dietary Exchanges:
Fruit ½
Starch ½

Rye

Move over, wheat! Foods made from rye may be less common, but their hearty flavor and numerous health benefits make them worth including in your meal plan.

nutrients per serving:

Rye Bread
1 slice

Calories 83
Protein 3g
Total Fat 1g
Saturated Fat 0g
Cholesterol 0mg
Carbohydrate 15g
Dietary Fiber 2g
Sodium 211mg
Potassium 53mg
Calcium 23mg
Iron 0.9mg
Thiamin 0.14mg
Riboflavin 0.1mg
Folate 35mcg

benefits

Like other whole grains, rye products—such as traditional rye bread and pumpernickel—are rich in fiber that helps keep blood sugar from skyrocketing following a meal. Compared to regular wheat bread, rye bread has also been shown to trigger less of an insulin response, so blood sugar is less likely to plunge, too. And as an added bonus, rye foods keep you feeling satisfied longer, making it easier to manage your appetite between meals and help you lose those extra pounds.

selection and storage

Rye grains may be available whole, cracked or rolled but are generally ground into flour. Rye flour comes as light rye flour, which has most of the bran (fiber) removed, while dark rye flour retains most of the bran and germ, so it has more fiber and nutrients. Store rye grains in an airtight container in a cool, dry, dark place, where they will keep for several months. Rye bread is available in the bread section of the supermarket.

preparation and serving tips

Rye bread is generally more compact and dense than wheat bread, so it works well for toasting or for sandwiches with hearty and moist fillings. Whole rye should be soaked overnight and will take longer to cook than cracked rye. It can be served like rice in soups, stews and stir-fries.

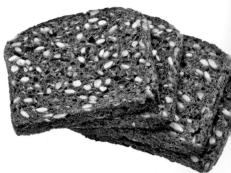

bran and honey rye breadsticks

1½ cups warm water (110°F)
1 package (¼ ounce) active dry yeast
1 teaspoon sugar
3¾ cups all-purpose flour, divided
1 tablespoon vegetable oil
1 tablespoon honey
½ teaspoon salt
1 cup rye flour
½ cup whole bran cereal
½ cup fat-free (skim) milk

1. Combine water, yeast and sugar in large bowl; let stand 5 minutes or until bubbly.

2. Add 1 cup all-purpose flour, oil, honey and salt. Beat with electric mixer at medium speed 3 minutes. Stir in rye flour, bran cereal and 2 cups all-purpose flour or enough to make moderately stiff dough.

3. Turn out onto lightly floured surface. Knead about 10 minutes, adding enough remaining flour to make smooth and elastic dough. Place in greased bowl; turn over to grease surface. Cover with damp cloth; let rise in warm place 40 to 45 minutes or until dough doubles in bulk.

4. Spray two baking sheets with nonstick cooking spray. Punch dough down. Divide into 24 equal pieces on lightly floured surface. Roll each piece into 8-inch rope. Place on prepared baking sheets. Cover and let rise in warm place 30 to 35 minutes or until dough doubles in bulk.

5. Preheat oven to 375°F. Brush breadsticks with milk. Bake 18 to 20 minutes or until golden brown. Remove to wire racks to cool completely.

Makes 24 servings

nutrients per serving:

Calories 104
Calories from Fat 9%
Protein 3g
Carbohydrate 21g
Fiber 1g
Total Fat 1g
Saturated Fat <1g
Cholesterol <1mg
Sodium 53mg

Dietary Exchanges:
Starch 1½

Salmon

Whether enjoyed as a main dish, on top of a salad or in a sandwich, salmon is rich in flavor and beneficial nutrients, making it a great alternative to the more typical whitefish.

nutrients per serving:

Salmon, farmed Atlantic
3 ounces roasted

Calories 175
Protein 19g
Total Fat 10g
Saturated Fat 2g
Cholesterol 54mg
Carbohydrate 0g
Dietary Fiber 0g
Sodium 52mg
Potassium 326mg
Calcium 13mg
Iron 0.3mg
Phosphorus 214mg
Selenium 35.2mcg
Niacin 6.8mg

benefits

Salmon may be a fatty fish, but most of the fat is omega-3s, healthy polyunsaturated fatty acids. Omega-3 fish oil helps protect against heart disease, a common diabetes complication, and has also been shown to improve the body's ability to respond to insulin. Omega-3s may also stimulate secretion of leptin, a hormone that helps regulate food intake, body weight and metabolism. Because a diet that includes fatty fish is so consistently associated with a variety of health benefits, the U.S. dietary guidelines recommend that we all eat fish twice a week.

selection and storage

Salmon is classified as either Pacific or Atlantic. There is only one species of Atlantic salmon, but there are five species of Pacific: chinook (king), sockeye (red), coho (silver), pink and chum. Whenever possible, choose wild rather than farm-raised salmon. Most Atlantic salmon is farmed. Some salmon are richer and fattier than others, but it is heart-healthy fat, so there is no need to worry. Look for fresh salmon with flesh that is firm to the touch. Fresh salmon is available whole or in steak or fillet form. Salmon is also available frozen, canned, dried or smoked.

preparation and serving tips

Salmon can be grilled, baked, broiled or steamed. It is naturally moist and tender and requires little seasoning, but a light sauce, such as teriyaki or honey mustard, complements the rich flavor.

salmon burgers with tarragon aioli sauce

Tarragon Aioli Sauce

- ⅓ **cup fat-free sour cream**
- 1½ **tablespoons reduced-fat mayonnaise**
- 1 **tablespoon fat-free (skim) milk**
- ½ **teaspoon dried tarragon**
- ¼ **teaspoon salt**
- ⅛ **teaspoon black pepper**

Burgers

- 1 **vacuum-sealed pouch (6 ounces) pink salmon**
- ¼ **cup plain dry bread crumbs**
- ⅓ **cup chopped green onions**
- ¼ **cup chopped fresh cilantro**
- 2 **egg whites**
- 2 **tablespoons lime juice**
- ⅛ **teaspoon ground red pepper**
   Nonstick cooking spray
- 4 **lime wedges**

1. Combine Tarragon Aioli Sauce ingredients in small bowl. Refrigerate until ready to use.

2. Combine burger ingredients in medium bowl.

3. Spray large nonstick skillet with cooking spray; heat over medium heat. Spoon equal amounts of salmon mixture into four mounds in skillet; flatten each mound. Cook 3 minutes on each side or until golden. Serve with Tarragon Aioli Sauce and lime wedges.

Makes 4 servings

nutrients per serving:

Calories 142
Calories from Fat 25%
Protein 15g
Carbohydrate 10g
Fiber 1g
Total Fat 4g
Saturated Fat 1g
Cholesterol 34mg
Sodium 316mg

Dietary Exchanges:
Starch 1
Meat 1½

Sesame Seeds

These tiny seeds may go unnoticed, but they add a nutty, slightly sweet taste and a delicate crunch to many dishes. Sesame seeds will boost the nutrient content, too.

benefits

Sesame seeds are low in calories but rich in beneficial minerals, including magnesium, calcium and potassium, which help maintain healthy blood pressure. This is especially valuable to people with diabetes in helping to reduce their heart disease and stroke risks. Among all nuts and seeds, sesame seeds have one of the largest amounts of cholesterol-lowering phytosterols, as well.

selection and storage

Sesame seeds come unhulled or hulled.

Unhulled, or whole, seeds retain their outer shell and can be brown, red or black. Hulled seeds have had their outer shell removed and are usually white or light yellow. Store unhulled sesame seeds in an airtight container in a dry, cool, dark place. Hulled sesame seeds need to be stored in the refrigerator. Sesame oil is available as plain or toasted and adds intense flavor to the foods it's cooked with.

preparation and serving tips

Sesame seeds are the primary ingredient in tahini (sesame seed paste), which is a main component in the popular Middle Eastern spread hummus. You can add sesame seeds to homemade breads or muffins. They also add a nice crunch and flavor when sprinkled on steamed vegetables, stir-fries or salads. Toasting sesame seeds intensifies their flavor. Try combining toasted sesame seeds with rice vinegar, tamari and crushed garlic for a dressing for salads, vegetables or noodles.

nutrients per serving:

Sesame Seeds, unhulled
½ ounce

Calories 80
Protein 2g
Total Fat 7g
Saturated Fat 1g
Cholesterol 0mg
Carbohydrate 4g
Dietary Fiber 2g
Sodium 0mg
Potassium 65mg
Calcium 140mg
Iron 2.1mg
Magnesium 50mg
Copper 0.4mg
Phosphorus 90mg

spiced sesame wonton crisps

20 (3-inch) wonton wrappers, cut in half
1 tablespoon water
2 teaspoons olive oil
½ teaspoon paprika
½ teaspoon ground cumin or chili powder
¼ teaspoon dry mustard
1 tablespoon sesame seeds

1. Preheat oven to 375°F. Spray two baking sheets with nonstick cooking spray.

2. Cut each halved wonton wrapper into two strips; place in single layer on prepared baking sheets.

3. Combine water, oil, paprika, cumin and mustard in small bowl; mix well. Brush evenly onto wonton strips; sprinkle evenly with sesame seeds.

4. Bake 6 to 8 minutes or until lightly browned. Remove to wire rack to cool completely. *Makes 8 servings*

nutrients per serving:

Calories 75
Calories from Fat 24%
Protein 2g
Carbohydrate 12g
Fiber <1g
Total Fat 2g
Saturated Fat <1g
Cholesterol 3mg
Sodium 116mg

Dietary Exchanges:
Starch 1

Soy Nuts

For a lower-calorie way to enjoy the flavor and crunch of eating nuts, try soy nuts. Soy nuts are similar in texture and taste to peanuts but are much lower in fat and higher in protein.

benefits

For people with diabetes, soy nuts are a great alternative to other nuts. Because soy nuts are generally lower in calories and fat, they're a better fit when you need to lose excess weight. And their larger protein and fiber loads make them easier on blood sugar. Plus, soy nuts pack isoflavones, powerful phytonutrients that help fight heart disease, a common complication of diabetes. Soy nuts are also rich in potassium, which may help lower the elevated blood pressure that often accompanies diabetes.

nutrients per serving:

Soy Nuts, dry roasted without salt 1 ounce

Calories 132
Protein 10g
Total Fat 7g
Saturated Fat 1g
Cholesterol 0mg
Carbohydrate 9g
Dietary Fiber 5g
Sodium 0mg
Potassium 410mg
Calcium 39mg
Iron 1.1mg
Folate 59mcg
Magnesium 41mg
Vitamin E <1mg

selection and storage

Packaged soy nuts may be oil or dry roasted and salted or unsalted. Flavors may be added, such as barbeque or smoked flavorings. They also may be found covered in yogurt or chocolate. Store in a cool, dry place for up to six months. Once the package is opened, store in an airtight container.

preparation and serving tips

Soy nuts make a great snack alone or combined with fiber-packed cereals, dried fruits and other nuts. They can be used as a crunchy topping for salads, too. To make soy nuts at home, soak dried soybeans in water for 6 to 8 hours, then drain and spread them in a single layer on an oiled baking sheet. Roast at 350°F for 30 to 50 minutes or until well browned, stirring often.

crunchy-fruity snack mix

1 cup roasted, salted soy nuts
1 cup halved pretzel sticks
⅔ cup dried cranberries
⅔ cup dried pineapple, cut into
    ½-inch pieces
⅔ cup white chocolate chips

Combine all ingredients in large bowl.

Makes 16 servings

Serving Suggestions: Try Crunchy-Fruity Snack Mix alone or on hot or cold cereals for breakfast. Sprinkle it on waffles or pancakes or use it as an ice cream topper. Also try it in baked goods, like muffins, quick breads or cookies.

nutrients per serving:

Calories 110
Calories from Fat 35%
Protein 3g
Carbohydrate 17g
Fiber 1g
Total Fat 4g
Saturated Fat 2g
Cholesterol 0mg
Sodium 60mg

Dietary Exchanges:
Fruit ½
Starch ½
Meat ½
Fat ½

Spaghetti Squash

People with diabetes can easily enjoy a heaping bowl of their favorite comfort food without any guilt. Spaghetti squash is a great substitute for carbohydrate-rich pasta, as its flesh separates into spaghetti-like strands when cooked.

nutrients per serving:

Spaghetti Squash
½ cup cooked

Calories 21
Protein 1g
Total Fat 0g
Saturated Fat 0g
Cholesterol 0mg
Carbohydrate 5g
Dietary Fiber 1g
Sodium 15mg
Potassium 90mg
Calcium 16mg
Iron 0.3mg
Vitamin A 85 IU
Vitamin C 3mg
Folate 6mcg

benefits

Although not as nutrient-rich as other winter squash, spaghetti squash has a place in a diabetic diet. It's a superb stand-in for regular pasta: It supplies far fewer calories, so it's better for your waistline, and it contains only about a third of the carbohydrates, so it has less effect on your blood sugar. Its fiber can keep you feeling full for longer, works to lower blood cholesterol levels and helps to even out blood sugar levels.

selection and storage

Spaghetti squash is often available year-round with a peak season from early fall through winter. It is oblong and usually bright yellow in color. Choose squash that is hard and smooth with an even color. Avoid greenish squash, which may not be ripe, and squash with bruises or signs of damage. Store uncut spaghetti squash at room temperature for several weeks.

preparation and serving tips

To prepare spaghetti squash, cut it in half lengthwise and remove the seeds. Because it can be hard to cut a raw squash, you can briefly cook the whole squash in the microwave to help soften it. After removing the seeds, cook until the flesh is tender and strands of squash are easily separated, 8 to 10 minutes in the microwave or 45 minutes to 1 hour in a 350°F oven. Then simply remove and separate the spaghetti-like strands from the shell with a fork and serve with desired sauces and toppings.

spaghetti squash primavera

1 teaspoon olive oil
¼ cup sliced mushrooms
¼ cup sliced green onions
¼ cup diced zucchini
¼ cup diced carrot
¼ cup diced green bell pepper
2 cloves garlic, minced
1 plum tomato, diced
1 tablespoon red wine or water
½ teaspoon dried basil
¼ teaspoon salt
⅛ teaspoon black pepper
2 cups hot cooked spaghetti squash
2 tablespoons grated Parmesan cheese

1. Heat oil in medium skillet over low heat. Add mushrooms, green onions, zucchini, carrot, bell pepper and garlic; cook and stir 10 to 12 minutes or until crisp-tender.

2. Stir in tomato, wine, basil, salt and black pepper; cook 4 to 5 minutes, stirring occasionally. Serve vegetables over spaghetti squash. Top with Parmesan cheese.

Makes 2 servings

nutrients per serving:

Calories 116
Calories from Fat 39%
Protein 5g
Carbohydrate 15g
Fiber 5g

Total Fat 5g
Saturated Fat 1g
Cholesterol 4mg
Sodium 396mg

Dietary Exchanges:
Vegetable 3
Fat 1

Spinach

Whether you eat it raw or cooked, spinach is a nutrition superstar that deserves a spot in a diabetic diet. However, cooked spinach is superior because it cooks down tremendously, making it an even more concentrated source of several nutrients and fiber.

benefits

Spinach is reasonably high in fiber, offering twice as much as most other cooking or salad greens. This calorie-free bulk fills you up and keeps you feeling full longer, a great advantage if you're pursuing weight loss to improve your condition. Spinach also contains the phytonutrient lipoic acid, which assists in energy production and may help regulate blood sugar. Where spinach really shines is as a source of essential antioxidants, vitamins A, C and E.

selection and storage

Choose spinach with leaves that are crisp and dark green; avoid limp or yellowing leaves. Refrigerate unwashed spinach in a loose plastic bag; it'll keep for three to four days. Prewashed bags of fresh spinach are readily available. Frozen or canned spinach is also a convenient option.

preparation and serving tips

Raw spinach makes for a wonderful salad—either on its own or mixed with other leafy greens. Chopped raw spinach can be added to many different dishes to boost the nutrient contents, such as soups, pasta sauces, casseroles or chilis. To serve cooked spinach as a side, simmer the leaves in a small amount of water for about 5 minutes or until the leaves begin to wilt. Top with lemon juice, seasoned vinegar, sautéed garlic or a dash of nutmeg.

nutrients per serving:

**Spinach
1 cup raw**

Calories 7
Protein 1g
Total Fat 0g
Saturated Fat 0g
Cholesterol 0mg
Carbohydrate 1g
Dietary Fiber 1g
Sodium 25mg
Potassium 165mg
Calcium 30mg
Iron 0.9mg
Vitamin A 2,813 IU
Vitamin C 8mg
Vitamin E 0.6mg
Folate 58mcg

greek chicken & spinach rice casserole

Nonstick cooking spray
1 cup finely chopped onion
1 package (10 ounces) frozen chopped spinach, thawed and squeezed dry
1 cup uncooked quick-cooking brown rice
1 cup water
¼ teaspoon salt
⅛ teaspoon ground red pepper
¾ pound chicken tenders
2 teaspoons dried Greek seasoning (oregano, rosemary and sage mixture)
½ teaspoon salt-free lemon-pepper seasoning
1 tablespoon olive oil
1 lemon, cut into wedges

1. Preheat oven to 350°F. Spray large ovenproof skillet with cooking spray; heat over medium heat. Add onion; cook and stir 2 minutes or until translucent. Add spinach, rice, water, salt and red pepper. Stir until well blended. Remove from heat.

2. Place chicken on top of mixture in skillet in single layer. Sprinkle with Greek seasoning and lemon-pepper seasoning. Cover with foil. Bake 25 minutes or until chicken is no longer pink in center.

3. Remove foil. Drizzle oil evenly over top. Serve with lemon wedges.   *Makes 4 servings*

nutrients per serving:

Calories 334
Calories from Fat 15%
Protein 26g
Carbohydrate 45g
Fiber 6g

Total Fat 6g
Saturated Fat <1g
Cholesterol 49mg
Sodium 535mg

Dietary Exchanges:
Starch 3
Meat 2

Split Peas

Split peas are a small but nutritionally mighty member of the legume family. Pea pods are harvested when they are fully mature; once dried, the peas split naturally.

nutrients per serving:

Split Peas
½ cup cooked

Calories 116
Protein 8g
Total Fat 0g
Saturated Fat 0g
Cholesterol 0mg
Carbohydrate 21g
Dietary Fiber 8g
Sodium 0mg
Potassium 355mg
Calcium 14mg
Iron 1.3mg
Vitamin A 7 IU
Folate 64mcg

benefits

Like beans and lentils, split peas are rich in protein but contain virtually no fat and far fewer calories than most animal sources of protein.

And they are a very good source of fiber, which helps to lower the commonly elevated cholesterol levels of people with diabetes. Furthermore, the fiber can aid diabetes management more directly by helping to prevent blood sugar spikes after a meal. They also provide decent amounts of potassium to support healthy blood pressure and folate to help protect the more vulnerable diabetic heart.

selection and storage

Split peas are usually found in packages or in bulk and may also be available whole. Most often they are green, but a yellow variety is also available. Store dried peas in an airtight container in a cool, dark place for several months. They can be refrigerated for longer.

preparation and serving tips

Before preparing dried peas, inspect and remove any debris or dirt. Split peas do not need to be presoaked like other legumes. To cook them, place in a saucepan with 3 cups of water for each cup of peas. Bring to a boil, then cover and simmer for about 30 minutes. Split pea soup is the most popular way this legume is eaten. Try adding split peas to vegetable soups or serve them with your favorite herbs and spices for a hearty side dish.

split pea soup

1 package (16 ounces) dried green or
  yellow split peas
7 cups water
1 pound smoked ham hocks *or* 4 ounces
  smoked sausage links, sliced and
  quartered
2 carrots, chopped
1 onion, chopped
½ teaspoon dried basil
¼ teaspoon dried oregano
¼ teaspoon black pepper

1. Rinse peas in colander under cold running water; discard any debris or blemished peas.

2. Combine all ingredients in large saucepan or Dutch oven; bring to a boil over high heat. Reduce heat to medium-low; simmer 1 hour 15 minutes or until peas are tender, stirring occasionally. Stir frequently near end of cooking time.

3. Remove ham hocks; let stand until cool enough to handle. Remove ham from hocks; chop. Discard bones.

4. Place 3 cups soup in blender or food processor; blend until smooth. (Or use hand-held immersion blender.)

5. Return to saucepan; stir in ham. If soup is too thick, add water until desired consistency is reached. Cook just until heated through.   *Makes 8 servings*

Note: To purée soup, carefully pour the hot mixture into the blender. Cover with the lid, removing the center cap, then cover the hole with a towel. Start blending at low speed and gradually increase to high speed, blending until desired consistency is reached.

nutrients per serving:

Calories 270
Calories from Fat 13%
Protein 24g
Carbohydrate 37g
Fiber 15g
Total Fat 4g
Saturated Fat 1g
Cholesterol 25mg
Sodium 640mg

Dietary Exchanges:
Starch 2½
Vegetable ½
Meat 1½

Strawberries

For people with diabetes, it may be difficult to find something to satisfy a sweet tooth. Juicy strawberries can do the trick and need no extra sweeteners or toppings. They are a great low-calorie, fiber-filled treat that can stand in for unhealthy desserts and snacks.

benefits

Strawberries are rich in a variety of phytonutrients that protect the heart and assist in blood sugar control. Recent research found that the polyphenols in strawberries may have the ability to blunt a rise in blood sugar levels after consuming table sugar. Eating strawberries several times a week also appears to be associated with a lower risk of type 2 diabetes. Strawberries are an exceptional source of vitamin C; they contain more than oranges and grapefruit.

selection and storage

Look for plump strawberries that are ruby red, evenly colored and have green, leafy tops. Avoid those that appear mushy or bruised. Bigger does not equal better; in fact, smaller berries tend to be the sweetest. Avoid strawberries in containers with juice stains or berries packed tightly with plastic wrap. Strawberries spoil quickly; it's best to serve them within a couple days of purchasing.

preparation and serving tips

Though they are delicious on their own, strawberries can perk up several types of dishes. Add some sliced strawberries to your bowl of cereal or yogurt or serve on top of a spinach salad. Add overripe strawberries to smoothies or fruit drinks or purée them for a sauce for fruit salads or desserts. Add a splash of balsamic vinegar to bring out their sweet flavor.

nutrients per serving:		
Strawberries 1 cup halves	**Total Fat** 0g	**Calcium** 24mg
	Saturated Fat 0g	**Iron** 0.6mg
	Cholesterol 0mg	**Vitamin A** 18 IU
	Carbohydrate 12g	**Vitamin C** 89mg
Calories 49	**Dietary Fiber** 3g	**Folate** 36mcg
Protein 1g	**Sodium** 0mg	
	Potassium 235mg	

strawberry granita

1 quart fresh strawberries, sliced
¼ cup powdered sugar
¼ cup water
2 tablespoons sugar substitute*
1 tablespoon fresh lemon juice, divided
   Fresh mint leaves (optional)
   Lemon peel strips (optional)

*This recipe was tested with sucralose-based sugar substitute.

1. Combine strawberries, powdered sugar, water, sugar substitute and lemon juice in blender; blend until smooth.

2. Pour into 8-inch square baking pan. Cover with foil and freeze 2 hours or until slushy. Stir to break into small chunks. Cover and freeze 2 hours. Stir to break up again. Cover and freeze at least 4 hours or overnight.

3. Scrape surface with large metal spoon; spoon into individual bowls. Garnish with mint and lemon peel. Serve immediately. *Makes 8 servings*

nutrients per serving:

Calories 54
Calories from Fat 0%
Protein <1g
Carbohydrate 14g
Fiber 1g
Total Fat 0g
Saturated Fat 0g
Cholesterol 0mg
Sodium 1mg
Dietary Exchanges:
Fruit 1

Sunflower Seeds

Sunflower seeds are a tasty gift from the beautiful sunflower. The kernels make a wonderful snack and provide an array of protective nutrients.

benefits

Sunflower seeds are an excellent source of vitamin E, an essential vitamin with antioxidant and anti-inflammatory effects that help protect the heart and reduce the risk of diabetic complications. The phytosterols found in sunflower seeds are natural cholesterol-lowering compounds, which is important for those with diabetes who also suffer from heart disease. Additionally, sunflower seeds contain mostly unsaturated fat, which can further help lower cholesterol, especially when it replaces the saturated fat abundant in many other snack foods.

selection and storage

Sunflower seeds are sold shelled or unshelled, salted or unsalted and dry or oil roasted. For less fat and sodium, choose unsalted dry roasted seeds. When purchasing unshelled seeds, look for firm, clean, unbroken shells. When purchasing shelled seeds, avoid those that appear yellowish in color. Sunflower seeds are high in fat, making them prone to rancidity. Therefore, they should be stored in an airtight container in the refrigerator or freezer.

preparation and serving tips

Besides being a great snack, a handful of sunflower seeds can lend crunch and flavor to many different foods. Try adding them to green salads, tuna or chicken salads, stir-fries or dips. Sprinkle them on hot or cold cereals or use them in a recipe to make your own energy bars or trail mix. They also can be baked into muffins, cookies, breads or rolls.

---

nutrients per serving:

Sunflower Seeds, kernels, dry roasted without salt
½ ounce

Calories 82
Protein 3g
Total Fat 7g
Saturated Fat 0.5g
Cholesterol 0mg
Carbohydrate 3g
Dietary Fiber 1.5g
Sodium 0mg
Potassium 120mg
Calcium 10mg
Iron 0.5mg
Vitamin A 1 IU
Vitamin E 3.7mg
Folate 34mcg

crunchy asparagus

- 1 package (10 ounces) frozen asparagus cuts
- 2 tablespoons water
- 1 teaspoon lemon juice
- 3 to 4 drops hot pepper sauce
- ¼ teaspoon salt (optional)
- ¼ teaspoon dried basil
- ⅛ teaspoon black pepper
- 2 teaspoons sunflower kernels
- Lemon slices (optional)

Microwave Directions

1. Place asparagus and water in 1-quart microwavable casserole dish; cover. Microwave on HIGH 4½ to 5½ minutes or until asparagus is hot, stirring once to break apart. Drain.

2. Combine lemon juice, hot pepper sauce, salt, if desired, basil and black pepper in small bowl. Pour over asparagus; toss to coat. Sprinkle with sunflower kernels. Garnish with lemon slices.

Makes 4 servings

nutrients per serving:

Calories 29
Calories from Fat 27%
Protein 2g
Carbohydrate 4g
Fiber 1g
Total Fat 1g
Saturated Fat <1g
Cholesterol 0mg
Sodium 4mg

Dietary Exchanges:
Vegetable 1

Sweet Potatoes

This tasty tuber shouldn't only be eaten at Thanksgiving. Rich in flavor and nutrients, sweet potatoes have much to offer in a diabetic diet.

benefits

The carotenoids in sweet potatoes appear to help stabilize blood sugar levels; they lower insulin resistance by making cells more responsive to the hormone. These effects not only aid in disease management but also make it easier to drop any excess pounds, which tend to aggravate the disease. Sweet potatoes also offer fiber to keep you full. Furthermore, their hefty nutrient load can help protect your heart and the rest of your body from damage and complications related to diabetes. For example, they supply infection-fighting vitamin C and blood pressure-lowering potassium.

selection and storage

Though often called a yam, a sweet potato is a different vegetable. Look for sweet potatoes that are small to medium in size with smooth, unbruised skins. Though sweet potatoes look rather tough and hard, they're actually quite fragile and spoil easily. Any cut or bruise on the surface quickly spreads, ruining the whole potato. Store them at room temperature, as refrigeration will speed up deterioration.

preparation and serving tips

Boil, bake or microwave unpeeled sweet potatoes. Leaving the peel intact prevents excessive loss of important nutrients and locks in the natural sweetness. Try sweet potatoes mashed, roasted or in a pie or soufflé. Use them to add moistness, flavor and plenty of nutrients to quick breads or muffins.

nutrients per serving:

Sweet Potato
½ cup flesh cooked

Calories 90
Protein 2g
Total Fat 0g
Saturated Fat 0g
Cholesterol 0mg
Carbohydrate 21g
Dietary Fiber 3.5g
Sodium 35mg
Potassium 475mg
Calcium 38mg
Iron 0.7mg
Vitamin A 19,218 IU
Vitamin C 20mg
Folate 6mcg

thyme-scented roasted sweet potatoes and onions

2 unpeeled sweet potatoes (about 1¼ pounds)

1 medium sweet or yellow onion, cut into chunks

2 tablespoons canola oil

1 teaspoon dried thyme

½ teaspoon salt

½ teaspoon smoked paprika

⅛ teaspoon ground red pepper (optional)

1. Preheat oven to 425°F. Spray 15×10-inch jelly-roll pan with nonstick cooking spray.

2. Cut sweet potatoes into 1-inch chunks; place in large bowl. Add onion, oil, thyme, salt, paprika and red pepper, if desired; toss to coat. Spread in single layer in prepared pan.

3. Bake 20 to 25 minutes or until very tender, stirring after 10 minutes. Let stand 5 minutes before serving. *Makes 10 servings*

nutrients per serving:

Calories 78
Calories from Fat 32%
Protein 1g
Carbohydrate 13g
Fiber 2g

Total Fat 3g
Saturated Fat <1g
Cholesterol 0mg
Sodium 148mg

Dietary Exchanges:
Starch 1
Fat ½

Swiss Chard

This leafy vegetable, with its crinkly green leaves and celery-like stalks, is a member of the beet family. And it may offer unique benefits for blood sugar regulation.

benefits

An array of phytonutrients in Swiss chard may help to prevent blood sugar from spiking after a meal by blocking the breakdown of carbohydrates into sugars. The fiber and protein in Swiss chard also help to keep blood sugar on a more even keel by regulating the speed of digestion. And Swiss chard is loaded with antioxidant nutrients, including vitamins A and C, which help protect the body's cells from stress and inflammation.

selection and storage

Swiss chard is available year-round but is best during summer months. The leaves may either be smooth or curly, while the stalks and veins range in color from red to yellow to creamy white. Look for leaves that are deep green without any browning or yellowing. Stalks should be crisp and without blemishes. Store Swiss chard in a sealed plastic bag in the refrigerator for up to five days. You can also blanch the leaves and freeze them.

preparation and serving tips

Wash Swiss chard under running water just before cooking. Stack the leaves and slice until you reach the stems. Cut stems into ½-inch slices, discarding the bottom. To bring out the sweetness of Swiss chard, boil the leaves and stems, then use in almost any type of dish, including pastas, omelets, frittatas and soups. Or you can simply enjoy it as a side dish, sautéed with olive oil, lemon juice and garlic.

swiss chard flavor packet

2 to 2½ pounds Swiss chard
1 cup diced onion
1 cup diced red bell pepper
½ cup diced carrot
½ cup chopped fresh cilantro or parsley
3 tablespoons fresh lime juice
1 tablespoon minced garlic
1 tablespoon olive oil
¼ teaspoon salt
¼ teaspoon black pepper

1. Preheat oven to 350°F. Tear 20×16-inch sheet of heavy-duty foil. Place on cookie sheet and spray with nonstick cooking spray. Remove stalks and large ribs from chard leaves. Cut stalks and ribs into ½-inch dice. Roll chard leaves into bundles and chop.

2. Toss chard, onion, bell pepper, carrot, cilantro, lime juice, garlic, oil, salt and pepper in large bowl.

3. Place chard mixture on center of prepared foil; roll and crimp edges upwards to make a packet. Bake 25 to 35 minutes. *Makes 6 servings*

nutrients per serving:

Calories 64
Calories from Fat 42%
Protein 3g
Carbohydrate 9g
Fiber 3g

Total Fat 3g
Saturated Fat 0g
Cholesterol 0mg
Sodium 378mg

Dietary Exchanges:
Vegetable 1
Fat ½

Tangerines

A type of mandarin orange, tangerines are intensely sweet and juicy. They pass easily as a dessert or treat, making them great for people with diabetes. Try the closely related clementine if you want to skip the seeds.

nutrients per serving:

**Tangerine
1 medium**

Calories 47
Protein 1g
Total Fat 0g
Saturated Fat 0g
Cholesterol 0mg
Carbohydrate 12g
Dietary Fiber 1.5g
Sodium 0mg
Potassium 145mg
Calcium 33mg
Iron 0.1mg
Vitamin A 599 IU
Vitamin C 24mg
Folate 14mcg

benefits

Tangerines fit nicely into a diabetes meal plan. They're wonderfully sweet yet supply only 47 calories and 12 grams of carbohydrate apiece, so they're a great substitute for typical treats, which are often loaded with calories, fats and carbohydrates. Plus, tangerines are a decent source of soluble fiber to help stabilize blood sugar and lower blood cholesterol levels. And while tangerines contain a third as much vitamin C and folate as oranges do, they provide three times as much disease-fighting vitamin A.

selection and storage

Tangerines are at their peak from November through June. Choose fresh tangerines that feel heavy for their size with smooth, unblemished skins. They should feel soft but not mushy. Store in the refrigerator for up to a week. Other varieties of mandarin oranges include the clementine, satsuma orange and honey tangerine. Most of the canned mandarin oranges are the satsuma variety.

preparation and serving tips

Tangerines, as well as other mandarins, are great when enjoyed on their own but are easy to prepare for other uses, like in salads. Just peel the fruit, separate the segments and pull off the membrane from the segments, if desired. Be sure to remove the seeds. Try adding tangerine segments to coleslaws or tuna salads. To get a boost of vitamins and minerals, try freshly squeezed tangerine juice; it is a great addition to salad dressings and marinades.

Tea

Whether iced or hot, tea is the most popular beverage worldwide. Its popularity is partly due to the discovery of an array of potential health benefits.

benefits

Drinking 2 to 3 cups of tea a day could offer several benefits for people with diabetes. Research shows that compounds in tea may improve the activity of insulin, potentially resulting in lower blood sugar. And antioxidants in tea may play a role in warding off diabetes complications, including cataracts and heart disease. Studies also suggest that tea may help suppress the growth of harmful bacteria that can cause infections, to which people with diabetes are more susceptible.

selection and storage

All teas (except herbal) come from the leaves, stems and buds of the *Camellia sinensis* plant. The difference is in how they are processed. White tea is derived from the new leaves in early spring. Green tea is from leaves that are dried right after harvesting. Black and oolong teas are partially dried, crushed and fermented to varying degrees. All types come either loose or in tea bags and should be stored in a cool, dark place. Be aware that instant, bottled and herbal teas do not offer the same health benefits.

preparation and serving tips

White and green teas should be brewed at a lower temperature (140°F to 180°F) than oolong and black teas (195°F). For the best flavor and maximum nutritional benefits, steep tea for 3 to 5 minutes. Honey, sugar, lemon or milk can be added to enhance flavor but also add calories.

nutrients per serving:

**Tea, black
1 cup brewed**

Calories 2
Protein 0g
Total Fat 0g
Saturated Fat 0g
Cholesterol 0mg
Carbohydrate 1g
Dietary Fiber 0g
Sodium 5mg
Potassium 90mg
Iron 0.1mg
Folate 12mcg

Tofu

Although tofu may be bland in flavor, this soybean by-product can aid in diabetes management. It is quite versatile—it takes on the flavors of what it's cooked with—so it can be a component in almost any dish.

benefits

Tofu is an excellent substitute for higher-fat meats—it offers high quality protein but is lower in calories and saturated fat, making it a wise choice if you need to lose weight to improve blood sugar control. Tofu's antidiabetes benefits may extend further. Some research suggests soy products may help lower blood sugar levels. Additionally, soy products have been found to be easier than animal protein on the vulnerable kidneys of people with diabetes. Soy protein also appears to help lower levels of damaging LDL cholesterol. And soy's isoflavones and other phytonutrients have been linked to a reduced risk of heart disease.

selection and storage

Tofu is made by curdling the milky liquid that is extracted from ground, cooked soybeans. It is available in regular or the smoother silken form. Both forms can be found in soft, firm or extra-firm textures. Firmer tofu is usually higher in fat. Tofu can be found refrigerated, packed in water, or unrefrigerated in aseptically sealed packages. Once opened, it should be kept covered with water in a container in the refrigerator. Changing the water daily will keep tofu fresh for up to one week. Unopened packages can be frozen for up to five months.

preparation and serving tips

Tofu can be served in a variety of ways, from salad dressings and dips to entrées and desserts. It has a neutral taste, which gives tofu the ability to absorb the flavors of other ingredients.

nutrients per serving:

Tofu, regular
½ cup

Calories 94
Protein 10g
Total Fat 6g
Saturated Fat 1g
Cholesterol 0mg
Carbohydrate 2g
Dietary Fiber 0.5g
Sodium 10mg
Potassium 150mg
Calcium 434mg
Iron 6.7mg
Vitamin A 105 IU
Folate 19mcg

eggless egg salad sandwich

1 box (16 ounces) firm tofu, drained, pressed* and crumbled
1 large stalk celery, finely diced
2 green onions, minced
2 tablespoons minced fresh parsley
¼ cup plus 1 tablespoon fat-free mayonnaise
3 tablespoons sweet pickle relish
2 teaspoons fresh lemon juice
1 teaspoon prepared mustard
  Black pepper, to taste
10 slices whole wheat bread, toasted
1½ cups alfalfa sprouts
10 tomato slices

*Stack two paper towels; fold in half and wrap around tofu. Repeat with another two-ply layer of paper towels so all sides are covered. Place wrapped tofu on a plate and cover with another plate weighed down with a heavy skillet so that tofu is firmly pressed. Allow tofu to rest 30 minutes in refrigerator so that paper towels absorb excess moisture.

1. Combine tofu, celery, green onions and parsley in large bowl. Whisk mayonnaise, relish, lemon juice, mustard and pepper in small bowl. Add to tofu mixture; mix well.

2. Divide mixture evenly among five bread slices. Top with alfalfa sprouts, tomato slices and remaining bread slices. Serve immediately.

Makes 5 servings

nutrients per serving:

Calories 229
Calories from Fat 24%
Protein 13g
Carbohydrate 34g
Fiber 5g

Total Fat 6g
Saturated Fat 1g
Cholesterol 0mg
Sodium 485mg

Dietary Exchanges:
Starch 2½
Meat ½

Tuna

Canned tuna may be one of the most commonly consumed fish, but don't miss out on the wonderful flavor and meatlike texture of fresh tuna.

benefits

Canned or fresh, tuna is a super source of protein, and regularly including it in your diet is a great way to get the omega-3 fats that experts recommend everyone get at least twice a week. Omega-3s can help fight the increased risk of cardiovascular disease that comes with diabetes. The omega-3 polyunsaturated fats in tuna help protect the heart by preventing erratic heart rhythms, making blood less likely to clot inside arteries, improving the ratio of "good" HDL cholesterol to "bad" LDL cholesterol and promoting healthy blood pressure.

selection and storage

Common varieties of tuna include yellowfin, which is deep red in color, and albacore, which is pale pink. Canned tuna usually indicates that it is light tuna (usually yellowfin) or white tuna (albacore). Canned tuna may be packed in water, broth or oil. For fewer calories and fat, choose water-packed tuna. Fresh tuna is available as steaks, fillets or pieces. Fresh tuna should be used within a day or two, or it can be tightly wrapped and frozen for up to a month.

preparation and serving tips

The ever-popular tuna salad can be lightened up by using fresh lemon juice, olive oil and a little mustard in place of mayonnaise. Consider nutritious add-ins, such as leeks, fennel, peppers, carrots, fruit and nuts. Fresh tuna steaks can be marinated and grilled or broiled for a tasty main dish or to top a mixed green salad.

nutrients per serving:

Tuna, canned in water 3 ounces			
Calories 109	Carbohydrate 0g	Iron 0.8mg
Protein 20g	Dietary Fiber 0g	Selenium 56mcg
Total Fat 2.5g	Sodium 40mg	Phosphorus 184mg
Saturated Fat 0.5g	Potassium 200mg	Vitamin B$_{12}$ 1mcg
Cholesterol 36mg	Calcium 12mg	

pan-seared tuna with spicy horseradish sauce

½ cup fat-free sour cream
1 tablespoon water
2 teaspoons prepared horseradish
1 teaspoon Dijon mustard
1 clove garlic, minced
½ teaspoon dried rosemary
½ teaspoon salt
4 fresh tuna steaks (4 ounces each),
    rinsed and patted dry
2 teaspoons no-salt-added steak
    seasoning blend
  Nonstick cooking spray
2 tablespoons finely chopped fresh
    parsley or green onion

1. Combine sour cream, water, horseradish, mustard, garlic, rosemary and salt in small bowl; set aside.

2. Sprinkle both sides of tuna with seasoning blend, pressing to adhere.

3. Spray grill pan with cooking spray; heat over medium-high heat. Cook tuna 1½ minutes on each side. Serve with sauce and parsley. *Makes 4 servings*

nutrients per serving:

Calories 198
Calories from Fat 27%
Protein 29g
Carbohydrate 6g
Fiber <1g

Total Fat 6g
Saturated Fat 1g
Cholesterol 48mg
Sodium 398mg

Dietary Exchanges:
Vegetable 1
Meat 3

Turkey Breast

Lean and rich in protein, turkey breast no longer needs to be served just at Thanksgiving dinner; it makes a great center of a meal any day of the year.

nutrients per serving:

Turkey Breast, skinless 3 ounces roasted

Calories 115
Protein 26g
Total Fat 0.6g
Saturated Fat 0.2g
Cholesterol 71mg
Carbohydrate 0g
Dietary Fiber 0g
Sodium 44mg
Potassium 248mg
Zinc 1.5mg
Iron 1.3mg
Vitamin B$_6$ 0.5mg
Vitamin B$_{12}$ 0.3mcg
Selenium 27mcg

benefits

Skinless turkey breast is among the leanest of meats, giving people with diabetes an alternative to skinless chicken breast as a way to get high quality protein with little saturated fat. Turkey breast is actually lower in fat than chicken, and as long as low-fat cooking and serving methods are used, it can fit quite easily in a diabetic meal plan. Turkey breast also contributes essential vitamins and minerals, including potassium for healthy blood pressure and zinc to promote wound healing and immune health.

selection and storage

Instead of buying a whole turkey, look for packages of breast meat. Feel free to prepare it with the skin on, which will lock in the juices and is also less expensive. Ground turkey breast is an option, but you'll want to read the label carefully as some ground turkey products also include dark meat, which will be higher in calories and fat. Turkey breast luncheon meat is lean and convenient. Store wrapped fresh turkey in the coldest section of your refrigerator and use within two to three days. Turkey breast can also be kept frozen.

preparation and serving tips

To keep lean turkey breast moist, cook it with the skin on and then remove the skin before eating. Turkey breast can be grilled, roasted or baked; it's done when the internal temperature reaches 165°F. Ground turkey breast is a great substitute for ground beef and works well in burgers, chilis, meat loaves, tacos and virtually any other recipe calling for ground beef.

Turnips

For a hearty side dish that is lower in blood sugar-raising carbohydrates than potatoes, go for turnips. Both the greens and the bulb of this economical and healthy vegetable are edible.

benefits

Unlike other root vegetables, turnips are relatively low in carbohydrates and provide a decent amount of soluble fiber. This combination helps fill you up for few calories and helps to prevent an upward spike in blood sugar after you eat. The soluble fiber also acts like a sponge to soak up cholesterol, helping to protect the vulnerable heart and blood vessels. In addition, turnips offer vitamin C, which promotes a healthy immune system to combat the increased susceptibility to infection associated with diabetes. The low-calorie greens are a source of heart-protective beta-carotene.

selection and storage

Turnips are available year-round, but the best ones are found in the fall. Baby turnips are the most tender and sweet and can be eaten whole, including their leaves. Turnips come in yellow-, orange- and red-fleshed varieties as well as white-fleshed. Look for turnips with smooth skins that are free of blemishes. Store in the refrigerator crisper drawer and use within a week or so.

preparation and serving tips

To prepare turnips, first remove the leaf end and root end. Larger turnips should be peeled, but smaller turnips can be cooked with the peel on. They can be boiled, baked, braised or steamed. Add turnips to stews, soups or vegetable dishes or mash them as a side dish. Baby turnips can be eaten raw. Turnip greens have a pungent flavor that becomes mild after cooking. Sauté the greens with olive oil and garlic for a savory side dish.

nutrients per serving:

Turnips
½ cup cooked

Calories 17
Protein 1g
Total Fat 0g
Saturated Fat 0g
Cholesterol 0mg
Carbohydrate 4g
Dietary Fiber 1.5g
Sodium 10mg
Potassium 140mg
Calcium 26mg
Iron 0.1mg
Vitamin C 9mg
Folate 7mcg

Walnuts

Compared to other nuts, walnuts provide the most omega-3 fats. Eating a handful of them daily is a delicious way to battle diabetes.

nutrients per serving:

**Walnuts, dry roasted without salt
1 ounce**

Calories 185
Protein 4g
Total Fat 18.5g
Saturated Fat 1.5g
Cholesterol 0mg
Carbohydrate 4g
Dietary Fiber 2g
Sodium 0mg
Potassium 125mg
Calcium 28mg
Iron 0.8mg
Folate 28mcg
Magnesium 45mg
Vitamin E 0.2mg

benefits

Eaten in moderation, walnuts are especially helpful for people with type 2 diabetes. They've been shown to reduce common dangerous characteristics of the disease, including insulin resistance, excess body weight and increased risk of heart disease. Walnuts provide a hefty amount of alpha-linolenic acid, the plant-based source of omega-3 fats that helps prevent blood clotting, reduce inflammation and lower triglyceride levels in the blood. Walnuts also supply protein and soluble fiber—a combination of nutrients that helps to satisfy hunger, lower cholesterol and smooth out blood sugar fluctuations.

selection and storage

Walnuts are most often available shelled but can also be purchased in the shell. Look for walnut shells without cracks or stains. Shelled walnuts are available whole, chopped or ground and should be crisp rather than limp or rubbery; check the freshness date before buying them. Store shelled walnuts in the refrigerator to prevent rancidity. In the shell, walnuts can be stored in a cool, dry place for up to six months.

preparation and serving tips

Walnuts can be enjoyed out of hand or chopped and added to many different foods. Toasting walnuts brings out the flavor. You can add them to homemade granola or use them to top oatmeal, cereal or yogurt. They are a wonderful addition to salads and vegetable dishes, as well. And their uses in muffins, pancakes, quick breads and cookies are endless.

french lentil salad

1½ **cups dried lentils, rinsed and sorted**
¼ **cup chopped walnuts**
4 **green onions, finely chopped**
3 **tablespoons balsamic vinegar**
2 **tablespoons chopped fresh parsley**
1 **tablespoon olive oil**
¾ **teaspoon salt**
½ **teaspoon dried thyme**
¼ **teaspoon black pepper**
4 **lettuce leaves (optional)**

1. Place lentils in large saucepan; add enough water to cover by 2 inches. Bring to a boil over high heat. Cover; reduce heat to low and simmer 30 minutes or until lentils are tender, stirring occasionally. Drain.

2. Meanwhile, preheat oven to 375°F. Spread walnuts in even layer on baking sheet. Bake 5 minutes or until lightly browned. Cool completely on baking sheet.

3. Combine lentils, green onions, vinegar, parsley, oil, salt, thyme and pepper in large bowl. Cover and refrigerate 1 hour or until cool.

4. Serve on lettuce leaves, if desired. Top with toasted walnuts before serving.

Makes 4 servings

Water Chestnuts

With its skin on, the water chestnut looks like a regular chestnut that's fallen from a tree. But in actuality, the water chestnut is a crunchy, juicy tuberous vegetable that comes from a water plant.

nutrients per serving:

Water Chestnuts
½ cup raw

Calories 60
Protein 1g
Total Fat 0g
Saturated Fat 0g
Cholesterol 0mg
Carbohydrate 15g
Dietary Fiber 2g
Sodium 9mg
Potassium 362mg
Calcium 7mg
Phosphorus 39mg
Magnesium 14mg
Vitamin C 3mg
Folate 10mcg

benefits

This unassuming vegetable adds a hint of sweetness for very few calories to a variety of Asian-inspired dishes. The water chestnut's fiber and protein contents help counter the blood sugar-raising effects of its carbohydrates—an obvious plus for people with diabetes. This combination also makes dishes that contain water chestnuts even more satisfying. Water chestnuts are very low in sodium and a good source of potassium and magnesium, two minerals that help to regulate blood pressure, making them useful for those with diabetes who also suffer from heart disease.

selection and storage

Water chestnuts are available fresh in most Asian markets. Choose those that are firm with no signs of shriveling. They should be stored tightly wrapped in the refrigerator and used within one week. Peel off their brownish black skin before using raw or cooked. Canned water chestnuts are readily available either sliced or whole. Be sure to rinse canned varieties before cooking to get rid of excess sodium.

preparation and serving tips

A staple in many Asian cuisines, water chestnuts are most often used in stir-fries; however, they can have many other uses. Add them to lettuce-based salads for extra crunch. Or chop them and add to tuna or chicken salads or veggie dips. Try them cooked with vegetables, such as asparagus or green beans.

southwestern chicken salad

Salad

- 1 can (about 15 ounces) no-salt-added black beans, rinsed and drained
- 12 ounces cooked boneless skinless chicken breasts, chopped
- 1 can (8 ounces) diced water chestnuts
- ½ red bell pepper, diced
- ½ green bell pepper, diced
- ¼ red onion, chopped
- ½ cup chopped fresh cilantro
- ½ jalapeño pepper,* minced (optional)

Dressing

- 3 tablespoons cider vinegar
- 2 tablespoons olive oil
- 2 tablespoons orange juice
- 1 teaspoon ground cumin
- ½ teaspoon chili powder
- ½ teaspoon ground red pepper
- ¼ teaspoon salt

Jalapeño peppers can sting and irritate the skin, so wear rubber gloves when handling peppers and do not touch your eyes.

1. Combine salad ingredients in large bowl; mix well.

2. Combine dressing ingredients in small container with tight-fitting lid. Shake until salt dissolves. Pour over salad; mix well.   *Makes 6 servings*

nutrients per serving:

Calories 188
Calories from Fat 30%
Protein 20g
Carbohydrate 15g
Fiber 5g

Total Fat 6g
Saturated Fat 1g
Cholesterol 44mg
Sodium 284mg

Dietary Exchanges:
Starch 1
Meat 2

Wheat Berries

Wheat berries are whole, unprocessed kernels of wheat. They're a nutritious substitute for rice and just as easy to prepare. Cooked wheat berries have a chewy bite and subtle nutty, earthy flavor.

benefits

Because they are unrefined, wheat berries retain all of their naturally occurring nutrients, including a decent amount of protein and a hefty amount of tummy-filling fiber. Wheat berries are especially useful for people with diabetes because the fiber slows the digestion of food and absorption of sugar, helping to prevent sudden blood sugar spikes. They are also a good source of magnesium and potassium, which may help to lower the elevated blood pressure often experienced by people with diabetes. And this whole grain provides a decent amount of niacin, which may be able to help increase blood levels of beneficial HDL cholesterol.

selection and storage

Wheat berries are often available in bulk bins in the natural foods section of the supermarket. They are usually labeled as "spring wheat" or "winter wheat," based on the time of year the wheat was sown. Most wheat berries are considered hard wheat, which is higher in protein. Hard wheat berries may be ground into whole wheat flour. Store wheat berries in a cool, dry place.

preparation and serving tips

Before cooking, rinse wheat berries under cool running water. Add them to boiling water and simmer for about 1 hour. (Allow for room as they will double in volume.) Add cooked wheat berries to soups and salads, serve them with sautéed vegetables as a side dish, or use them in a holiday stuffing.

nutrients per serving:

Wheat Berries
½ cup cooked

Calories 158
Protein 7g
Total Fat 0.5g
Saturated Fat 0g
Cholesterol 0mg
Carbohydrate 33g
Dietary Fiber 6g
Sodium 0mg
Potassium 163mg
Calcium 12mg
Iron 1.7mg
Magnesium 60mg
Selenium 34mcg
Niacin 2.7mg

fennel wheat berry salad

- 3 cups water
- ½ cup wheat berries
- 2 tablespoons balsamic vinegar
- 1 tablespoon olive oil
- 1 tablespoon honey
- 1¼ teaspoons whole fennel seeds, toasted*
- 3 cups coleslaw mix

*To toast fennel seeds, spread in single layer in small skillet. Cook and stir over medium heat 1 minute or until seeds are golden. Remove from skillet immediately.

1. Combine water and wheat berries in medium saucepan; bring to a boil over high heat. Reduce heat to low; cover and simmer 1 hour or until wheat berries are tender. Drain. Place wheat berries in large bowl; cover and refrigerate at least 1 hour.

2. Whisk vinegar, oil, honey and fennel seeds in small bowl. Add coleslaw mix to wheat berries. Drizzle with dressing; toss to coat. Serve immediately.   *Makes 6 servings*

Tip: For a more colorful salad, choose a coleslaw mixture that contains both green and red cabbage.

nutrients per serving:

Calories 81
Calories from Fat 33%
Protein 2g
Carbohydrate 13g
Fiber 2g
Total Fat 3g
Saturated Fat <1g
Cholesterol 0mg
Sodium 102mg

Dietary Exchanges:
Vegetable 1
Starch ½
Fat ½

Wheat Bran

Literally bursting with fiber, wheat bran—the hard outer shell of the wheat kernel—offers an easy way to boost the fiber in almost anything you eat.

nutrients per serving:

Wheat Bran
½ cup

Calories 63
Protein 5g
Total Fat 1g
Saturated Fat 0g
Cholesterol 0mg
Carbohydrate 19g
Dietary Fiber 12g
Sodium 0mg
Potassium 345mg
Magnesium 177mg
Iron 3.1mg
Zinc 2.1mg
Niacin 3.9mg
Vitamin B6 0.4mg

benefits

Wheat bran is a great tool for increasing fiber intake as it can easily be incorporated into several foods. And for people with diabetes, eating a fiber-rich diet, filled with whole grains, fruits and vegetables, is essential for keeping blood sugar within a healthier range. Fiber-rich foods play an important role in weight loss, too, which is important for those with diabetes who need to lose weight to improve their condition. Wheat bran also contributes heart-protective nutrients, such as niacin, which may boost HDL, or "good," cholesterol levels, and potassium and magnesium, which help lower blood pressure.

selection and storage

Wheat bran is usually available in bulk bins in the natural foods section of the supermarket, or it may be found with grains or cereals. Wheat bran is best stored in an airtight container in the refrigerator for prolonged shelf life.

preparation and serving tips

Wheat bran can be added to foods to boost the fiber contents. Sprinkle it over hot or cold cereals, yogurt or applesauce. Add wheat bran to breads, cookies, muffins and pancakes. It can be added to ground meat dishes, such as meat loaves or casseroles. Toasting wheat bran gives it a nutty flavor and crunchy texture.

Yellow Squash

A type of summer squash, yellow squash is also known as crookneck squash because of its swanlike neck.

benefits

Yellow squash's thin skin, tender seeds, small stock of carbohydrates and high water content together aid in diabetes control. This winning combination helps to keep post-meal blood sugar levels from spiking and provides a fullness that makes it easier to skip seconds. Yellow squash also contains vitamin C and beta-carotene, antioxidants that may play a role in fighting heart disease. It is also rich in folate, which appears to lower the level of homocysteine, a substance that can damage blood vessels. Plus, the vitamin C can help fight inflammation and ward off infections, which are more common in people with diabetes.

selection and storage

Yellow squash is at its peak during summer months but is available year-round. It should feel heavy for its size and have shiny, unblemished skin. Look for summer squash that is small to average in size. Larger yellow squash may have harder skin and tends to have larger seeds and stringy flesh. It is very perishable and should be stored unwashed in a plastic bag in the refrigerator for up to five days.

preparation and serving tips

Wash yellow squash under cool running water and then cut off both ends. It can be sliced into rounds and enjoyed raw with a dip or grated into thin strips and added to a fresh salad. Sauté yellow squash with onions, bell peppers, eggplant and tomatoes to make the delicious side dish ratatouille.

nutrients per serving:

Yellow Squash
½ cup cooked

Calories 21
Protein 1g
Total Fat 0g
Saturated Fat 0g
Cholesterol 0mg
Carbohydrate 3g
Dietary Fiber 1g
Sodium 0mg
Potassium 160mg
Calcium 20mg
Iron 0.3mg
Vitamin A 1,005 IU
Vitamin C 10mg
Folate 21mcg

Yogurt

Yogurt has a rich nutrient profile and can be enjoyed in several ways, making it an ally in diabetes management.

nutrients per serving:

Yogurt, plain low-fat 1 cup

Calories 154
Protein 13g
Total Fat 4g
Saturated Fat 2.5g
Cholesterol 15mg
Carbohydrate 17g
Dietary Fiber 0g
Sodium 170mg
Potassium 575mg
Calcium 448mg
Iron 0.2mg
Vitamin A 125 IU
Vitamin C 2mg
Folate 27mcg

benefits

Yogurt is great for people with diabetes. It's a nutrient-rich substitute for higher-calorie sugary desserts and provides satisfying protein to help battle hunger and even out blood sugar between meals and snacks. The protein content in yogurt allows it to easily be used in meals as a substitute for high-fat meats. And the live active bacteria cultures found in yogurt help with digestive health by suppressing the growth of harmful bacteria in the intestinal tract. These beneficial bacteria promote immune health, too. Stronger immune function may help counter the increased vulnerability to infections that comes with diabetes.

selection and storage

To keep fat and calories low, look for low-fat or nonfat yogurt. The addition of fruit or sweeteners adds calories, so look for plain varieties and add your own fruit or flavorings. Some yogurt products are sweetened with noncaloric sweeteners. Check for a "sell-by" date on the yogurt carton; it will keep for up to ten days past that date.

preparation and serving tips

Yogurt makes a great portable meal or snack on its own, but it has several other great uses. Yogurt makes a wonderful base for smoothies when blended with fresh fruit and juice. Or top your morning bowl of cereal with yogurt instead of milk. Yogurt is especially well suited as a base for dips and salad dressings or in place of mayonnaise in coleslaws and tuna or chicken salads.

frozen lemonade pie

1 cup graham cracker crumbs (about 7½ crackers, crushed)
1 cup plus 2 tablespoons sugar substitute,* divided
1 tablespoon margarine, melted
1 tablespoon canola oil
2 tablespoons egg white
2 cups plain nonfat yogurt
1 cup thawed reduced-fat whipped topping
Grated peel of 1 lemon
6 tablespoons lemon juice (2 medium lemons)
½ teaspoon lemon extract
2 to 3 drops yellow food coloring (optional)
Shredded lemon peel (optional)

This recipe was tested using sucralose-based sugar substitute.

1. Preheat oven to 350°F. Spray 9-inch pie pan with nonstick cooking spray.

2. Combine graham cracker crumbs, 2 tablespoons sugar substitute, margarine and oil in medium bowl. Add egg white; mix well.

3. Press crumb mixture on bottom and up side of prepared pan. Bake 8 to 10 minutes. Cool completely.

4. Meanwhile, whisk yogurt, whipped topping, remaining 1 cup sugar substitute, lemon peel, lemon juice, lemon extract and food coloring, if desired, in large bowl. Pour filling into cooled crust and smooth top. Lightly cover with plastic wrap and freeze 4 hours or until frozen.

5. Let stand 10 minutes before slicing. Garnish with shredded lemon peel. *Makes 8 servings*

nutrients per serving:

Calories 155
Calories from Fat 35%
Protein 6g
Carbohydrate 22g
Fiber <1g

Total Fat 6g
Saturated Fat 2g
Cholesterol 1mg
Sodium 202mg

Dietary Exchanges:
Starch 1½
Fat 1

Zucchini

Often mistaken for a cucumber, zucchini, a type of summer squash, has a high water content that makes it one of the lowest-calorie vegetables.

nutrients per serving:

Zucchini
½ cup cooked

Calories 14
Protein 1g
Total Fat 0g
Saturated Fat 0g
Cholesterol 0mg
Carbohydrate 2g
Dietary Fiber 1g
Sodium 0mg
Potassium 240mg
Calcium 16mg
Iron 0.3mg
Vitamin A 1,005 IU
Vitamin C 12mg
Folate 25mcg

benefits

With so little carbohydrate to spark a jump in blood sugar levels, zucchini gets an invitation to join its cousin, the yellow squash, as welcome regulars in a diabetic diet. Zucchini provides folate, an essential B vitamin, and generous doses of vitamins A and C, all of which can help protect the heart and blood vessels from cell damage that may lead to cardiovascular disease, a common diabetes complication. And zucchini's fiber can play a role in lowering elevated blood cholesterol levels, while its potassium can help maintain a steady heartbeat and keep blood pressure in check.

selection and storage

Zucchini is available year-round in most supermarkets. Look for smaller squash for the best flavor. The skin should be deep green with yellow speckles and it should be firm and unblemished. Zucchini should be stored in the refrigerator and used within a few days.

preparation and serving tips

The mild flavor of zucchini complements other ingredients in a variety of dishes. It is especially delicious sautéed with tomatoes and onions. Zucchini makes a tasty, colorful and nutritious addition to lasagnas, pasta sauces or stir-fries. The perfect way to use a larger zucchini is to grate it and bake it into a low-fat cake or quick bread, adding nutrition and moistness without any detectable flavor.

quick zucchini parmesan

- 2 teaspoons olive oil
- 2 large zucchini, cut into ¼-inch-thick slices (4 cups)
- 2 cloves garlic, minced
- ¼ teaspoon black pepper
- ¼ teaspoon salt (optional)
- ¼ cup thinly sliced fresh basil
- 2 tablespoons grated Parmesan cheese

Heat oil in large nonstick skillet over medium heat. Add zucchini; cook and stir 2 minutes. Add garlic, pepper and salt, if desired; cook and stir 4 to 5 minutes or until zucchini is tender. Top with basil and Parmesan cheese.

Makes 4 servings

nutrients per serving:

Calories 50
Calories from Fat 54%
Protein 2g
Carbohydrate 4g
Fiber 1g
Total Fat 3g
Saturated Fat <1g
Cholesterol 2mg
Sodium 48mg

Dietary Exchanges:
Vegetable 1
Fat ½

Glossary

Amino acids: the building blocks of protein. Twenty amino acids are necessary to help the body grow, repair itself and fight disease. Nine of these are considered "essential" because they must come from food you eat, while the body can produce the others.

Anthocyanins: a type of flavonoid responsible for the red and blue pigments found in certain fruits and vegetables. Anthocyanins can help prevent the growth of cancer, lower LDL "bad" cholesterol and prevent clots from forming.

Antioxidant: certain vitamins, minerals and enzymes that help protect cells from damage caused by oxidation, which can result from exposure to tobacco smoke, sunlight, radiation and pollution, as well as aging and illness. Antioxidants offer protection against heart disease, cancer, diabetes, eye disease and numerous other health conditions.

Beta-carotene: a potent antioxidant found in red, orange and yellow plant foods and in some dark green vegetables. It is converted to vitamin A in the body.

Carbohydrate: one of the three major nutrients in food, providing 4 calories per gram. Complex carbohydrates are the primary supplier of energy in the diet and can be found mainly in breads, cereals, pasta, potatoes, squash, beans and peas. Sugars are also known as simple carbohydrates and provide calories (and energy) with few nutrients.

Carotenoids: pigments that give foods their red, orange and yellow colors. Over 600 different carotenoids have been identified, some of which are powerful antioxidants, including beta-carotene, lutein and lycopene.

Cholesterol: a waxy substance produced by your liver that is part of every cell in the body. The body uses it to manufacture hormones and other essential substances. It is also supplied by the diet when you eat foods from animal sources. Some cholesterol is essential for life, but it can be dangerous as it builds up on artery walls, narrowing blood vessels. LDL (low density lipoprotein), or "bad," cholesterol deposits cholesterol in blood vessels, where it forms plaque that can lead to heart disease. HDL (high density lipoprotein), or "good," cholesterol helps remove cholesterol from the blood and delivers it to the liver, where it can be eliminated.

Cruciferous vegetables: a family of vegetables, including bok choy, broccoli, brussels sprouts, cabbage, cauliflower, kale, mustard greens and turnips, that have cancer-fighting properties. The family is named for its cross-shaped flowers.

Diabetic retinopathy: damage to the retina of the eye that results from poorly controlled blood sugar levels. It can lead to severe vision loss or even blindness.

Fat: one of the three major nutrients in food, providing 9 calories per gram. Saturated fats, found in butter, stick margarine, meat, poultry skin and whole-fat dairy foods, are solid at room temperature and can raise blood cholesterol levels. Unsaturated fats, found in vegetable oils, nuts, olives and avocados, are liquid at room temperature and help lower blood cholesterol levels.

Fiber: the parts of plants that cannot be digested. Insoluble fiber absorbs water and adds bulk to stools, easing elimination, promoting digestive regularity and providing a feeling of fullness after eating. Soluble fiber forms a gel in the digestive tract and slows the rate of digestion, which helps regulate blood sugar levels and prevent the absorption of cholesterol.

Flavonoids: health-protective substances found in the colorful skins of fruits and vegetables as well as in beverages such as tea, red wine and fruit juices. Their health benefits are similar to those of antioxidants.

"Free Food": any food or drink that contains less than 20 calories or 5 grams or less of carbohydrates per serving. For people with diabetes, small amounts of these foods can be enjoyed with little or no effect on blood sugar levels.

Glucose: the basic form of sugars and carbohydrates found in food. It is transported in the blood and used as the primary source of energy. Glucose in the blood is referred to as blood sugar.

Immune function: the body's ability to defend itself against disease and illness.

Insulin: a hormone made by the body that helps transfer glucose from the blood into cells, where it can be used as energy to fuel body functions.

Insulin resistance: the diminished ability of cells to respond to insulin, causing an increase in blood glucose levels. Insulin resistance forces the body to make more insulin in an attempt to transfer the excess glucose in the blood into the cells.

Legumes: edible seeds that grow in pods; includes beans, peas, lentils and peanuts.

Lutein: a pigment found in foods that are bright yellow, orange and green. Along with zeaxanthin, this carotenoid pigment is linked to a reduced risk of macular degeneration and cataracts.

Lycopene: a powerful antioxidant that gives numerous foods their red color and is especially abundant in tomatoes. It helps protect against prostate cancer, lung cancer and heart disease.

Macular degeneration: deterioration of the central portion of the retina that causes severe vision loss and even blindness, most often in people over 60. Certain nutrients, including vitamins C and E, beta-carotene, zinc and copper, can decrease the risk of vision loss.

Metabolic syndrome: a combination of conditions, including high blood pressure, high blood sugar, too much fat around the waist, low HDL cholesterol and high triglycerides, that tend to occur together and, when they do, increase the risk of type 2 diabetes, heart disease and stroke.

Omega-3 fats: a type of unsaturated fat essential for human health that is found in fish, including salmon, tuna and halibut. They are also found other seafood, including algae and krill, as well as in some plants and nut oils. These healthy fats play a critical role in brain function, as well as normal growth and development. They help to reduce inflammation that can lead to heart disease, cancer and arthritis.

Pectin: a soluble fiber that helps to lower artery-damaging LDL cholesterol. It is found in most plants but is most abundant in apples, cranberries, plums, grapefruits, lemons and oranges.

Plaque: the fatty substance that builds up in blood vessels. It can constrict blood flow and lead to heart attack and stroke.

Protein: one of the three major nutrients found in food, providing 4 calories per gram. It helps with cell growth and repair as well as fight disease. Vegetable sources include beans, nuts and whole grains. Animal sources include fish, poultry and meat.

Phytochemicals: another name for phytonutrients.

Phytonutrients: natural substances found in plants that help protect the plant from disease. In humans, phytonutrients have numerous health-promoting properties; they function as antioxidants to help rid the body of toxins and prevent inflammation.

Polyphenols: natural chemicals in plants, including fruits, vegetables, seeds, legumes and grains, that are responsible for much of their color, flavor and scent. They act as antioxidants and block enzymes that can promote cancer growth.

Triglycerides: the name for fat that travels in your blood, where it is transported to cells and used for energy. High levels of triglycerides can raise your risk of heart disease and may be a sign of metabolic syndrome.

U.S. Dietary Guidelines: official food and nutrition advice for Americans ages 2 and older, jointly published by the U.S. Department of Health and Human Services and the Food and Drug Administration. The guidelines are revised every 5 years, based on the latest scientific research on the effect of food and nutrients on health.

Zeaxanthin: a pigment found in foods that are bright yellow, orange and green. Along with lutein, this pigment in the carotenoid family is linked to a reduced risk of macular degeneration and cataracts.

Metric Conversion Chart

VOLUME MEASUREMENTS (dry)

$1/8$ teaspoon = 0.5 mL
$1/4$ teaspoon = 1 mL
$1/2$ teaspoon = 2 mL
$3/4$ teaspoon = 4 mL
1 teaspoon = 5 mL
1 tablespoon = 15 mL
2 tablespoons = 30 mL
$1/4$ cup = 60 mL
$1/3$ cup = 75 mL
$1/2$ cup = 125 mL
$2/3$ cup = 150 mL
$3/4$ cup = 175 mL
1 cup = 250 mL
2 cups = 1 pint = 500 mL
3 cups = 750 mL
4 cups = 1 quart = 1 L

VOLUME MEASUREMENTS (fluid)

1 fluid ounce (2 tablespoons) = 30 mL
4 fluid ounces ($1/2$ cup) = 125 mL
8 fluid ounces (1 cup) = 250 mL
12 fluid ounces ($1 1/2$ cups) = 375 mL
16 fluid ounces (2 cups) = 500 mL

WEIGHTS (mass)

$1/2$ ounce = 15 g
1 ounce = 30 g
3 ounces = 90 g
4 ounces = 120 g
8 ounces = 225 g
10 ounces = 285 g
12 ounces = 360 g
16 ounces = 1 pound = 450 g

DIMENSIONS

$1/16$ inch = 2 mm
$1/8$ inch = 3 mm
$1/4$ inch = 6 mm
$1/2$ inch = 1.5 cm
$3/4$ inch = 2 cm
1 inch = 2.5 cm

OVEN TEMPERATURES

250°F = 120°C
275°F = 140°C
300°F = 150°C
325°F = 160°C
350°F = 180°C
375°F = 190°C
400°F = 200°C
425°F = 220°C
450°F = 230°C

BAKING PAN SIZES

Utensil	Size in Inches/Quarts	Metric Volume	Size in Centimeters
Baking or Cake Pan (square or rectangular)	$8 \times 8 \times 2$	2 L	$20 \times 20 \times 5$
	$9 \times 9 \times 2$	2.5 L	$23 \times 23 \times 5$
	$12 \times 8 \times 2$	3 L	$30 \times 20 \times 5$
	$13 \times 9 \times 2$	3.5 L	$33 \times 23 \times 5$
Loaf Pan	$8 \times 4 \times 3$	1.5 L	$20 \times 10 \times 7$
	$9 \times 5 \times 3$	2 L	$23 \times 13 \times 7$
Round Layer Cake Pan	$8 \times 1 1/2$	1.2 L	20×4
	$9 \times 1 1/2$	1.5 L	23×4
Pie Plate	$8 \times 1 1/4$	750 mL	20×3
	$9 \times 1 1/4$	1 L	23×3
Baking Dish or Casserole	1 quart	1 L	—
	$1 1/2$ quart	1.5 L	—
	2 quart	2 L	—